# Seeing in the Dark

# Seeing in the Dark

## University Sermons

### NICHOLAS LASH

DARTON · LONGMAN + TODD

First published in 2005 by
Darton, Longman and Todd Ltd
1 Spencer Court
140–142 Wandsworth High Street
London
SW18 4JJ

Thanks are due to Gwydion Thomas for permission to quote
'Sea-Watching' by. R. S. Thomas (p. 22) originally published in
R. S. Thomas – Laboratories of the Spirit (London, 1975)
© Kunjana Thomas (2001).

ISBN 0 232 52619 2

A catalogue record for this book is available from the British Library.

Designed by Sandie Boccacci
Phototypeset by Intype Libra Ltd
Printed and bound in Great Britain by
Page Bros, Norwich, Norfolk

# Contents

## LIVING AND DYING

## GOD'S WORK

# Introduction

One of the pleasures of teaching theology in Cambridge is being invited to preach at Evensong (or, in the case of King's College, Matins) in college chapels. Seventeen of these sermons, preached between 1969 and 1996, were delivered in response to such invitations. Only five (numbers 1, 8, 10, 12 and 19) are university sermons in the strict sense of being 'sermons preached before the university of . . .'

I have not tried to update references to current affairs and preoccupations. Each of these sermons had a date, as well as a place: it seemed better to leave them as they are, rather than render them spuriously timeless. I have, however, rendered biblical quotations according to the New Revised Standard Version, which has the advantage of attempting inclusive language, and the disadvantage of mild anachronism, since this version was not published when many of these sermons were delivered.

Two pieces need a word of explanation. At the beginning of 'Enquiry and attentiveness', I speak of being 'doubly indebted' to John Hulse's benefaction. From this obsessive testator's numerous bequests there still survive an annual Hulsean prize essay, an annual series of Hulsean Lectures, an annual university sermon, and part of the stipend of the Norris-Hulse Professor of Divinity (a position which I had the privilege of occupying from 1978 to 1999). The Norris-Hulse chair was created, in 1934, from the amalgamation of the Hulsean chair with that deriving from another eighteenth-century benefaction: that of John Norris, a wealthy landowner, who was inspired by a sermon, delivered by the Bishop of London, deploring the poverty of doctrinal teaching in the England of the day.

From few people have I learnt as much as I did from David Woodard, a quite remarkably dedicated priest whose curate I had the privilege of being from 1963 to 1968. I was deeply touched by his request that I should preach at his requiem, and grateful to the Bishop of Northampton, Frank Thomas, for permission to do so (see 'The valley of bones').

The picture on the cover was chosen because I have tried, in a number of these pieces, to bring out the enduring centrality to Christian discipleship of the garden of Gethsemane. Moreover, the publisher found irresistible the image, on the cover of a book of sermons, of disciples fast asleep.

*Nicholas Lash*
*Cambridge, August 2005*

# HOPE

# 1

## Waiting for God: the integrity of expectation

If you are walking in remote hill-country – somewhere, perhaps, on the Yorkshire moors – and a mist comes up, and you lose your way, it may be sensible to take a few steps in this direction, backtrack, move a little distance in another direction, tentatively exploring a range of possibilities.

But, if you are really lost, badly lost, then there is sometimes only one thing left to do – and that is to set out resolutely in one direction and stick to it, refusing to be diverted from your path. This second strategy may turn out to be disastrous – but there are circumstances in which it is the least irrational option open to you.[1]

A modern Chancellor of the Exchequer, receiving irreconcilable advice from highly qualified teams of economic experts is, perhaps, faced with some such alternative. Should he explore, provisionally and tentatively, now this, now that solution or combination of solutions? Or should he, conscious of the fact that the conflictual character of the advice he receives is due, not to lack of competence on the part of his advisers, but to the uncontrollable range of largely unknown and unknowable economic variables, march out resolutely in one direction, pursue – inexorably – one line of policy until it bears fruit in either success or disaster?

I don't know. I have no competence in these matters. But I am clear that there are aspects of our human existence in respect of which the adoption of any such apparently heroic strategy of single-mindedness is not only inappropriate, but is incompatible with integrity.

Let me try to indicate what I have in mind. I assume – and

some of you may share the assumption – that ours is the pain or privilege of living at a time of profound cultural crisis. In our society there is no unquestioned assurance and agreement concerning the significance of human existence, the goals to be pursued, the values to be cherished, the means by which goals are to be secured or values established. We are lost, badly lost, in the fog.

We are not, however, alone. Out of the mist there appears a host of self-appointed guides, offering straightforward solutions to our dilemma, remedies for our bewilderment. Politically, they come both from the right and from the left; ideologically, they come in the starched white laboratory coats of secular humanism and the pseudo-oriental robes of a variety of forms of religion. I shall have something to say, later on, about some of these quack-doctors of a culture in crisis. For the moment, I simply want to register my conviction that the adoption of the remedies they offer is, in principle, incompatible with human and Christian integrity.

Today is the first Sunday in Advent. At this season, the mood of Christian worship focuses on the fact that Christian existence is human existence characterised and constituted as existence in *hope*, in expectation. If, as I have suggested, the times in which we live are times of profound uncertainty and upheaval – times of political, economic, cultural, moral and religious bewilderment – if we are, indeed, badly lost on the moor – then the celebration of Advent becomes a less straightforward affair than it may once have seemed to be. In times such as these, what are the available and appropriate forms of hope and expectation? How may we hope with integrity? There are, I suggest, two unacceptable forms of response to such questions.

The first unacceptable response is the 'realistic' one, which runs – roughly – as follows: Don't expect too much out of life. Settle for what you've got, or – at least – for what is within arm's reach. Ask not for definitive peace, unconquerable joy, the healing of all pain and isolation. To dream of the unattainable is only to make matters worse. Be realistic: settle for small joys, the partial reduction of violence, fragments of happiness.

William Blake once said: 'If any could desire what he is incapable of possessing, despair must be his eternal lot.'[2] The 'realist', as I have characterised him, *knows* that he is incapable of possessing what he also knows, but dare not admit, that he desires. The realist settles for despair masquerading as common sense. There is a strand in our literary tradition which would paint despair in noble, heroic colours. In fact, despair lacks nobility – it is counterfeit tragedy, carrion comfort, shrivelled and tawdry like all forms of egocentricity.

The other unacceptable type of response to questions concerning the appropriate form of hope and expectation is what – though the term may be somewhat misleading – I shall call the 'utopian' one. Utopianism comes in many guises, but they all have this – at least – in common: that the utopian, offering his services as guide in our bewilderment, stands beside us in the fog, points with complete assurance in one direction, and one direction only, and says: Look, can't you see – in *that* direction lies reality, daylight, homecoming.

All forms of utopianism – political and religious – have their sights set on distant invisible horizons; they scorn the detailed texture of the foreground, impatiently dismissing the complexities of our bewilderment as unimportant, illusory, unreal. There is, in this dismissal, an element of vulgarity, of insensitivity and – very often, from the Crusades to the Gulag archipelago – of sheer brutality. This element of brutality stems from the fact that the utopian knows too much about the future. Your utopian knows just what is going on and what the outcome will be. He is impatient of paradox, variety and uncertainty. He cannot tolerate alternatives. And, since the infinite complexity and irreducible variety of human experience and relationship, action and language, do not fit his simple vision, the simplicity of the vision is maintained by ignoring or riding roughshod over the unwelcome complexity of the facts – and the vast majority of the facts are men and women.

Teilhard de Chardin was one of those who knew too much about the future. There is a chilling abstractness about many of his comments, in his correspondence, on the Second World War. It comes as little surprise that a man who, in 1940, could write: 'too many, just now, are only weeping over their own small losses . . . the Germans deserve to win because, however bad or mixed is their spirit, they have more spirit than the rest of the world',[3] should have admitted, in 1927, that he could only overcome his 'antipathy' to human beings by looking 'at Man, either impersonally', or else 'personally', in (a suspiciously abstract) Christ.[4]

It is the selective, abstract insensitivity of the utopian response which renders it, or which should render it, unacceptable to the Christian: to the man or woman whose hope is grounded in the paradox and particularity of the ministry and death of one whose gentleness had nothing in common with weakness; whose integrity and unswerving obedience had nothing in common with the spurious single-mindedness of the one-track mind.

T. S. Eliot asked, in *Ash Wednesday*, 'Where shall the word be found, where will the word/Resound?' The utopian Christian, the confident guide – be he Teilhardian or totalitarian, dogmatist or fundamentalist – has no difficulty in answering that question; indeed, he answers it even before it is seriously asked. And if the answer he produces so readily, the words that tumble forth as soon as we so much as raise an eyebrow in interrogation, lack the wholeness, the healing power, of a Word that is spirit and life, this is perhaps because he does not wait for Mr Eliot to finish what he was saying:

'Where shall the word be found, where will the word/ Resound? Not here, there is not enough silence.' The hopefulness of Jesus, his sustained integrity, was not that of a man who could keep going because he knew the answers. The integrity of Jesus' expectation was the integrity of sustained attention to the silence of God. If our hope, as followers of Christ, is to have the same quality, it can only be through a renewed recognition that 'the primary business of prayer is to be attentive.'[5] Alan Ecclestone has said of Newman that 'the engagement he sought to bring about and the passion that inspired him belonged not to the argument he pursued, but to the silence in which the Yes to God must be articulated.'[6]

The 'discernment of spirits' is never easy, but there are few areas in which its exercise is currently more urgent than in the discriminating assessment of the 'variety of religious experience'.

As Christians, it is always incumbent upon us to give an account of the hope that is in us; to attempt an answer to the question: Why do you hope? Why do you suppose that much makes sense? To Christian thinkers of the eighteenth century, of the Enlightenment, it seemed that their predecessors had sought the warrants for their hope in the voices of authority: the authority of ecclesiastical authorities, the authority of revealed truth, the authority of the past. For the thinkers of the Enlightenment, however, the past had ceased, as such, to be authoritative. And so, instead of seeking authority for hope, they sought reasons for optimism.

But, just as the reasonableness of trusting the authority of the past was thus undermined and rendered questionable, so the authority of reason has, in turn, been discredited. We are no longer confident that we have reasons for optimism. We are no more able to hope merely because the logic of the arguments for hope is (formally) impeccable than we are able to hope merely because other people once hoped in the past.

But, if the past is too uncertain, and logic too fragile a guide, where should we turn? To what ground should we appeal in our attempts to answer the question: Why do you hope? Why do you suppose that much makes sense?

From the Romantic movement to our own day, it is increasingly to their *experience* that men and women have turned. It is only in the measure that the claims we make can be cashed in terms of our experience that they effectively persuade and sustain us.

The appeal to experience has, of course, a very long history, but it has adopted new forms and acquired a new centrality in our own day.

But to what do we refer when we speak of 'religious'

experience? One of the components of the remarkable
revival of interest, in recent years, in what is called 'religion',
seems to have been a growing and largely unquestioned
assumption that the concept of 'religious experience' stands
for a discriminable psychological state, alongside such states
as fear, and love, and hope and pain. In the quest for such
experience, through a variety of forms of spiritual techniques and religious associations, increasing numbers of
people seem to find meaning and identity, wholeness and a
sort of peace. But in what sense, and for whom, is such
wholeness and peace liberation rather than a reinforcement
of slavery? Confronted by a 'religious' revival which includes
such unpleasant phenomena as the Unification Church, the
flourishing – in an India wracked by poverty – of 'ashrams'
for wealthy Westerners, the recent tragedy in Guyana, it
would be grossly irresponsible not to press such questions.

The pedlars of 'religion' are currently amongst the most
vociferous of the utopian guides in our darkness. But where
are they leading us? A friend of mine was asked a few years
ago how, as a Christian theologian, he reacted to the
renewed interest in 'religion'. He replied: 'I don't know. I'm
not yet sure whether these are movements of hope or of
despair.'

For my part, I am increasingly convinced that, in their dissociation of 'sacred' from 'secular', of feeling from rationality, of spirit from matter, of satisfaction from responsibility,
many of these movements speak the accents of despair. Not
the least disturbing feature that many of them have in common is their radical egocentricity: 'religion', human experience of and contact with the mystery that some call God,
loses altogether that fundamental quality of attentiveness,
in darkness, to the silence of God, and becomes a set of
techniques for the self-satisfaction of human needs. We
seem a long way from the Sermon on the Mount and the
garden of Gethsemane.

Am I calling in question the appeal to experience as the
ground of human hope? By no means. But it is at least worth
considering whether the Christian, for whom the veil of the
temple between sacred and secular, religion and politics,

spirit and matter, is confessed to have been – in the historical enfleshment of God's Word and Spirit – torn down, should seek the experience of God elsewhere than in the particular mundane details of human experience.

The experience that grounds our human and Christian hope must be at once as universal and as particular as the entire range of human relationships and institutions, achievements and failures, joy and suffering. If experience is to give grounds for hope, it will only appropriately do so in the measure that we seek attentively to construe *all* our experience – whether domestic or political, scientific or social, aesthetic or sacramental – however darkly and paradoxically, as experience of God.

But is this possible? Can God so 'appear' in our experience as yet not, by his appearing, to do violence to our humanity? For the characters in Beckett's play, the *possibility* of Godot appearing is the one thing that makes the waiting, and the passage of time, less than totally absurd. And yet, if he were to appear, if the absolute were to irrupt into the texture of history, the form of his appearance would be demonic – the absolute could only appear, within history, crushing and doing violence to the fragility and particularity of historical existence. Or so it would seem; and so, contrary to their best intentions, have Christians frequently presented the incarnation of the Son of God.

And yet, however often Christians have distorted the image of the Lordship of Christ into the story of a theophany, an irruption of an other, a not-human, a cosmic giant in human disguise, it is not the appearance of such a Christ that we expect, in Advent. The first Christians, who had come to recognise, in the darkness of Good Friday, in the squalor of a provincial execution, the definitive act and presence of God, went on to recognise, in that weakness in the stable, the form of God's power.

Christian hope, as I understand it, refuses either of the two options that I have described as unacceptable – the 'realistic' and the 'utopian' – because both these options, the denial of the absolute and the dismissal or destruction of the complexity of the particular, are aspects of despair.

The peculiarity of Christian hope, whose verbal and symbolic expressions are necessarily paradoxical, is that it both expects that absolute healing which is, even now, the presence of God, while yet insisting that we take with complete seriousness, as problem and responsibility, each particular feature and facet of our bewilderment.

The German theologian Karl Rahner has said that 'The Christian has fewer "ultimate" answers which he could throw off with a "now the matter's clear" than anyone else.'[7] It is no part of the Christian hope to fly in the face of the evidence and to deny that we are lost, badly lost. If that hope is sustained, it is not by the conviction that we 'know the answers', that we are not 'really' lost, that there is – if only we would follow the guides – an obvious solution. Christian hope is sustained by the conviction, which is received and cannot, with integrity, be constructed at will, that, being lost, we are – nevertheless – being found.

PREACHED BEFORE THE UNIVERSITY OF LEEDS,<br>3 DECEMBER 1978

*Notes*

1. The late Professor Ernest Gellner can in no way be held responsible for the use (or misuse) I am making of an image which he powerfully deploys in the opening chapter of his study of *Legitimation of Belief* (Cambridge, 1974).
2. 'There is no Natural Religion', *William Blake: Selected Poetry*, ed. Michael Mason (Oxford, 1996), p. 36.
3. Teilhard de Chardin, *Letters to Two Friends, 1926–1952* (London, 1970), p. 146.
4. *Letters to Two Friends*, p. 63.
5. Alan Ecclestone, *Yes to God* (London, 1975), p. 16.
6. *Yes to God*, p. 19.
7. K. Rahner, *Christian at the Crossroads* (London, 1975), p. 23.

# 2

# Journeying in hope

Genesis 12:1–9
Hebrews 11:1–16

A prudent listener would not risk offering even the briefest of comments on our first reading before consulting the experts in these matters, and poring over the commentaries. In a fit of lamentable imprudence, I am afraid that I simply read the text. And reading it, with my naiveté untroubled by information, I was struck by the paradox of Abraham's journey.

He knew where he came from: from his own land and his father's house. And he knew why he was journeying: in obedience to God's command. And he knew that this journey, in obedience to God's command, was a necessary condition for the realisation of God's promise: the promise that he would, in a new and better land, be made into a 'great nation' (12:2), sustained and cherished by God.

But did he know *where* he was going? To this question, the structure of the narratives precludes any straightforward answer. The author of the Letter to the Hebrews lays great emphasis on Abraham's faith, his trust, his obedience, in going out, in journeying – 'not knowing where he was going' (11:8). And if we attend merely to the beginning and the end of the first reading, there is a disturbing bleakness about the direction of his pilgrimage. At the start, we hear of him leaving the warmth, and security, and comfort, of his homeland. At the end, we are told that he 'journeyed on by stages towards the Negeb' (12:9), the desert, the wilderness, the far country.

Along the way, however, he passes through the land of Canaan. And as he does so, the Lord appears to him and says: 'To your offspring I will give this land' (12:7). There is no suggestion that Abraham should break his journey and seek to take possession of the land. The journey continues, towards the wilderness, and the land of promise, glimpsed in passing, is left behind. The journey continues, towards the wilderness, and any attempt to depict its outcome, to anticipate – in the imagination – the fulfilment of the promise, is rendered impossible by the fact that the only glimpse afforded him now lies behind him. It is, surely, intensely paradoxical that the one episode which might illuminate the darkness of his hope as he journeys towards the wilderness is a brief incident which now belongs, irrevocably, to the past?

There are a number of different strategies which Christians employ in their attempts appropriately to co-ordinate memory and hope, past and future, in the negotiation of present experience.

For some, it seems that truthfulness and integrity can only be sustained by maintaining and strengthening the use of ancient symbols, the performance of ancient rites, the repetition of ancient words, the shoring up of ancient institutions. Without this fidelity of memory, the Gospel would be betrayed – supplanted by some other message, of our own ephemeral construction, designed to meet present needs and current standards of intelligibility and relevance.

For others, it seems that truthfulness and integrity can only be sustained by having the courage to break with the past for the sake of the future; by having the courage to admit that most of the things which Christians once believed have by now been rendered incredible; by having the courage to discard inherited possessions. Only by travelling light, unencumbered by the trappings of nostalgia, can we hope to be obedient to the command – to continue to journey towards the wilderness.

If I were forced simply to choose between the strategy of retention and the strategy of dispossession, thus described,

I would, I confess, find the choice difficult, for reasons that I shall indicate in a moment. But I have no doubt as to where the initial emphasis has to lie – and it is on the side of the strategy of dispossession. Discontinuity with our past is simply not an option. It is, in many respects, both a charge laid upon us and an ineluctable fact.

If we seek to cling to inherited possessions, to hang on to our past, we shall find that it has slipped through our fingers. Whether we like it or not, words change their meaning, institutions their function, customs their use. Moreover, preoccupation with the retention of the past ensures inattention to the demands of the present. A form of Christianity which is concerned, first and foremost, with retaining its inheritance, is likely to prove insensitive both to the demands of present suffering and to problems concerning its institutional and linguistic *insertion* in contemporary culture. In other words, contrary to the best intentions of its adherents, such a Christianity is likely to become, not a movement effectively concerned with the redemption of the human, with its liberating transformation in the direction of the promise, but an esoteric subculture. As such, it is likely to possess not even the virtue of irrelevance: more probably, it will fulfil a darker and more destructive social function. And if this seems an over-statement of the case, I would remind you of the character and social implications of those forms of Christian self-perception which contributed most actively to the electoral success of President Reagan.

Nevertheless, to lay the initial emphasis on the strategy of dispossession is not necessarily to set at naught the abiding significance of the past. Discontinuity with our past, I have suggested, is not an option but an ineluctable fact. If there is to be maintained identity, appropriately perceived continuity with our past, such continuity is to be discovered, received, again and again, as gift, not clung to as possession. This is as true of the history of the Church as it is of the growth and maturation of personal relationships.

If, however, the strategy of dispossession is correct in its central perception that it is only in losing our life that we find it, in going out from the warmth and security of a

known land that we journey, in darkness, towards the realisation of the promise, that strategy – as I have described it –
is nevertheless dangerously oversimplified. It proceeds as if
our tale could be told, our journey undertaken, simply in
terms of the beginning and the end of our first reading –
simply in terms of the movement from initial security
towards the wilderness.

But this is to forget the curious incident along the way –
that brief passage through the land of Canaan; the moment
(now past) at which the Lord appeared and said to
Abraham: 'To your offspring I will give this land' (12:7).

How does this episode fit into the story? I would like to
approach this question indirectly, by briefly considering
another: How do *creeds* arise, and what is their function in
the Christian scheme of things?

On one account, creeds arise as people begin to build
fantastic structures of speculation on the simple facts of
Jesus' life, teaching and death. And, once constructed, this
edifice of speculation distracts attention both from the fact
of Jesus and from the facts and demands of present experience: from the challenge of poverty, weakness and suffering
to present responsibility.

That the creed has often been thus construed, and that it
has often fulfilled such function, I do not deny. But I question this account of the origin of the creed, and I deny that
it necessarily serves such purposes.

I suggest that the creeds arose, in the first instance, as
Christians sought to make sense of their present experience
– individual, domestic and political – in the light of their
memory of the fact and perceived significance of Jesus the
Christ.

The language of belief is, for the Christian as for the Jew,
a language of attempted autobiography. Our story, the story
by which we attempt to make sense of our existence, of our
journey in history, begins (as does the Jewish story): 'My
father was a wandering Aramean.' But the Christian autobiography includes elements which the Jewish story does
not: it contains reference, constitutive of its narrative iden-

tity, to him who was born of the virgin Mary and suffered under Pontius Pilate.

The creed, I am suggesting, is the tersely abbreviated form of the Christian story (and the eucharistic prayers of most liturgical traditions retain this narrative character even more clearly than the creeds themselves). To be a Christian is to be able to tell this story as one's own: to make of this narrative one's own autobiography.

It is, however, of fundamental importance to notice that the story remains necessarily unfinished. We cannot, individually or corporately, *complete* the narrative so long as we continue on the journey. The story remains unfinished so long as the journey remains unfinished; so long as, individually and corporately, we continue to travel towards the wilderness, the desert of death.

It is, I suggest, this unfinished character that differentiates the language of hope from the languages of both optimism and despair. Both optimism and despair know the answer, are clear about the outcome: they prematurely complete the story. Both optimism and pessimism, utopianism and cynicism, are implicitly totalitarian: they know too much about the future. Whereas the language of hope, the language of an unfinished narrative, retains an interrogative character. The grammar of the language of hope includes assertive and descriptive elements. But these are, in the last resort, subordinate to the grammar of interrogation and request. Unless the confession of Christian faith, the telling of the Christian story, retains its fundamental character as prayer, it loses its identity. We have no way of describing or predicting the outcome of the journey; of discerning what lies ahead, in the wilderness.

Am I suggesting that, for the Christian, the future remains simply an 'open question'? No. The truth of the matter is more paradoxical than that. I am suggesting that, in the course of our journey, we passed briefly through a land of which it was said, as we passed through it: 'To your offspring I will give this land.' Bethlehem and Capernaum, Gethsemane and Jerusalem, are not far from Canaan. I am suggesting that the land of the promise has been briefly

glimpsed, pointed out to us, in the past. The journey continues, towards the wilderness, the unknown future and the
desert of death, and any attempt to depict its outcome, to
anticipate – in the imagination – the fulfilment of the promise, is rendered impossible by the fact that the only glimpse
afforded us now lies behind us. Or perhaps it might be better to say that we are, even as we journey, enabled to speak
of the outcome, but only in terms of that episode which
briefly illuminates the darkness of our hope.

To put it as simply as possible: the Christian narrative,
tersely summarised in the creed, is a story the focal point of
which remains the announcement of Christ's resurrection.
And this announcement of the transformation of death into
life is an announcement the grammar of whose utterance is
the grammar of prayer: of trustful request that it be made
true in the transformation of all weakness, all suffering, all
mortality.

I have been trying, in the light of our readings, impres-
sionistically to indicate why it is that Christian faith in God
and his promise necessarily retains the character of a venture, of a risk undertaken in obedience: not a 'leap', but a
pilgrimage. John Henry Newman always spoke of faith in
these terms. And to a correspondent who objected that the
concepts of 'risk' and 'venture' were quite inappropriate for
the characterisation of Christian faith, Newman replied:
'Did not Abraham, my dear Sir, make a venture, when he
went out, not knowing whither he went?'[1]

TRINITY COLLEGE, CAMBRIDGE,
16 NOVEMBER 1980

*Note*

1. John Henry Newman, *Letters and Diaries* vol. XII (London, 1962), p.
   168.

# 3

# Nostalgia

Job 19:1–9, 23–27a
1 Corinthians 15:1–8, 12–26

There are situations in which the intensity of pain, or pleasure, or concentration, is such that we find the present
moment totally absorbing. In such situations, it is misleading even to speak of 'present' experience, because the
absorption is such that there is no consciousness of past or
future, of the passage of time, in which to situate the
moment as 'present'.

But these are rare moments. Most of the time, neither the
pain, nor the pleasure, nor the concentration, is such as to
exercise so totalitarian a grip on our experience. Most of
the time, our experience *is* of experience in time, of movement from the past into the future.

And the present, thus experienced, is rarely satisfactory.
Or, at least, it can only be rendered satisfactory by closing
our minds and hearts to the suffering of others and to the
fearfulness and questionableness of our own existence. It
requires courage, and integrity, to 'look the present in the
face', because the face of the present is lined with savagery,
violence, loneliness and death. The face of the present
doesn't make sense: in it, the absence of pattern, and order,
and justice, threatens our rationality, our sanity, our identity. And from this darkness there is no escape.

And so, in the darkness, we seek freedom by attempting
to discern or to construct patterns of light. We do this by
prospecting, from our unfreedom, images of freedom in
the past or in the future. Nostalgia and revolutionary

utopianism are two of the devices we use in our attempts to make the present less intolerable.

Both devices are dangerous: to romanticise either the past or the future is to relate to a past or to a future which is unreal and, as unreal, is an evasion of the reality of the present.

To remember the past in happiness is by no means necessarily evasion: to do otherwise would often be morbid ingratitude.

But nostalgia goes further than this: it is a return to something we never had. This is why the revisiting of some place in which we once experienced great happiness can be so depressing, so disillusioning.

As Christians, as adherents of a religion in which the truths by which we live are so inextricably bound up with time and tradition, with particular people, places and circumstances, we are highly susceptible to the attractions of nostalgia. Hence our tendency to romanticise the 'primitive Church', or 'the ages of faith', or the 'purity of the Reformation', or whatever other time or place or climate of belief we may prefer to select in contrast to those features of the present – in Church or society – that we find intolerable.

But nostalgia is not the only device we employ in order to seek refuge from a present that we find intolerable or unacceptable. In a situation in which nothing makes sense, in which all meaning and value has been put in question, in which reality and power seem the prerogative of chaos, we also reconstruct the past in such a way as to enable us to perceive significance in the present.

If the past can be construed as the unfolding of a story which leads with perceptible inexorability to the present, the present takes on a more orderly and hence a more kindly appearance.

Our forebears in the nineteenth century were very good at doing this. They were very good at construing their present as the flowering of the process of history; a process which, it seemed, had taken place almost entirely for their benefit. This comfortable illusion was shattered by events which culminated in the First World War and the October Revolution.

Once again, as Christians, as adherents of a religion in which the truths by which we live are so inextricably bound up with time and tradition, we are peculiarly prone so to reconstruct the past as to provide us with patterns making sense of the present.

It may well be that, without some such attempt, it is impossible to sustain a coherent belief in divine providence. But we should at least be careful: careful of fantasising our past in order to enable us to evade the responsibilities and complexities of the present.

To perceive the past as a process which has taken place simply for our benefit is to falsify both past and present by refusing to accept the past on its own terms, as carrying its own meaning and significance, which may well not be ours.

I have in mind, for example, our tendency to read the Old Testament as a body of writings whose significance is only carried in the New, in our time, in the time of Christ.

Few passages in the Old Testament have been so frequently subjected to this treatment as that verse from the book of Job to which we listened just now: 'I know that my Redeemer lives' (Job 19:25a).

But, if I remind you that that was *not* what Job said, or intended, am I not guilty of that pedantry which made Erasmus, writing for his friend Sir Thomas More, refer to theologians as 'a remarkably supercilious and touchy lot'?[1] I don't think so.

What worries me is that, if we so misinterpret Job as to hear him speaking of the resurrection of Christ, we show no interest in Job himself. And I suggest that, if we would appropriately celebrate the resurrection of Christ, we would be advised to take an interest in Job's predicament.

Earlier in that same passage, Job had said of God: 'He has walled up my way so that I cannot pass' (19:8a). If there is a note of hope in the passage, taken as a whole, it is not an illusory, utopian hope, born of an inability to accept the intolerability of the present.

'He has walled up my way so that I cannot pass.' Job confronts his unfreedom, his present darkness. He does not pretend that things are more satisfactory, more 'meaning-ful', less darkly threatening than they appear to be.

'He has walled up my way so that I cannot pass.' Karl Barth said of this passage: 'Job is looking to the point where the obscurity of the divine rule encounters him at its most impenetrable, the approaching darkness of his being in death.'[2]

*In* that situation, not in evasion of it, he confessed his trust in God.

And in that situation, in that same approaching darkness, Jesus, in the pattern of his passion and death, confessed his trust in the Father.

'If Christ has not been raised, your faith is futile', said St Paul in our second reading (1 Corinthians 15:17a). It is that resurrection which at all times, but especially at this season, we confess and celebrate.

But, if our confession of faith in Christ's resurrection is to be, in the deepest sense, 'realistic', if it is truly to be the beginning of freedom, and the acceptance of responsibility to 'change the world', to work for the freedom of all in God, then it must be, not a fantasising evasion of the intolerabil-ity of the present, but – for us as for Job – the acceptance of a gift: the gift of a trust which refuses evasion even when, especially when, the obscurity of the divine rule is encoun-tered at its most impenetrable.

'The last enemy to be destroyed', says St Paul, 'is death' (15:26). And death is not destroyed by evasion, by nostalgia or by utopian fantasy, but by the power of God in which, by faith in Christ's resurrection, we share.

KING'S COLLEGE, CAMBRIDGE,
30 APRIL 1978

## Notes

1. Erasmus, *Praise of Folly*, trans. Betty Radice (London, 1974), p. 80.
2. Karl Barth, *Church Dogmatics* IV/3 (Edinburgh, 1961), p. 424.

# 4

## Watchfulness

Isaiah 52:1–12
1 Thessalonians 5

*Advent and electricity*

It would, I think, be a mistake to overlook the difference made by electricity to the celebration of Advent. I am not thinking of the way 'the market' pressures us to sell or celebrate or, at least, illuminate the advent of festivities in October. More serious than this is the fact that the contracting light, the deepening darkness, of early winter only means increased fuel bills and some inconvenience in collecting children from school. We do not *dread* the dark as those may do whose lives and livelihood are more directly shaped by daylight.

In the deepening dark before the solstice we do not, as it were, hold our breath, expectant of an annual miracle yet fearful lest it not occur: the coming as gift in winter of the unconquered sun, the turning that is the harbinger of spring. The quite straightforward connections of sense and story which led the Church to fix the celebration of the birth of Christ at this point of the year are lost on us, communicated only indirectly as fable or as allegory. When, therefore, we hear Paul telling us that we are children of light, not of the night or darkness, we have to interpret this, labour the connections out, behave like those dull people who kill the joke stone dead by requiring that its argument be spelt out.

I am not, for a moment, regretful of electric light and heat, for both of which – thank God! I only wish to suggest that the materials of our education into watchfulness, into appropriately Christian expectation of God's coming, do not lie as immediately to hand for us as they did for those who wrote the Scriptures and composed our liturgies. In calling us to expectation, to watchfulness, in the way that they do, Paul and Isaiah mean quite simply what they say. But, if we are to *hear* this, then we may sometimes need to take a detour through rather different territory.

## Sea-watching

Through North Wales, perhaps, where the priest and poet R. S. Thomas lives, and watches, on a windswept headland. Hour after hour, he watches the sea breaking on the shore. What is he expecting? What kind of coming, what manner of advent, does he await? The form of the question is not quite right: the important thing to notice is the manner of his watchfulness. Here is his own description:

> Grey waters, vast
>     as an area of prayer
> that one enters. Daily
>    over a period of years
> I have let the eye rest on them.
> Was I waiting for something?
>          Nothing
> but that continuous waving
>    that is without meaning
> occurred.
>    Ah, but a rare bird is
> rare. It is when one is not looking,
> at times one is not there
>         that it comes.
> You must wear your eyes out,
> as others their knees.
>    I became the hermit

of the rocks, habited with the wind
and the mist.[1]

### Presumption and despair

The stillness and solitude are central to the poem.

> Daily
> over a period of years
> I have let the eye rest on them.

Programmed as we are to confuse action with 'bustle', we
may almost be tempted to suppose that 'letting the eye rest'
is a kind of *in*activity, mere restfulness. Yet few things are
more strenuous, more demanding of time and discipline
and effort, than the kind of attentiveness, stillness, disinter-
est, watchfulness, which the poem describes.

The distinction to be drawn lies not, I think, between
action and passion, between 'doing things' and having
things done to one, but rather between behaving as if we
were the centre of the world and learning that we are not.

There are, moreover, two different ways of behaving as if
we were the centre of the world. We can act like lords of the
world or like its hapless victims.

As lordlings, energetic little Prometheans, we rush
around the place, controlling and explaining, constructing
and arranging, all manner of things: cities and arguments,
liturgies and local government, and (best of all) other people's lives.

As agent centres of the universe, we don't know the first
thing about watchfulness, because all watchfulness is, quite
obviously, a waste of time: what on earth would *we*, the
world-makers, be watching *for?*

In its Christian guises, this besetting energetic egotism
talks of 'seeking' or 'finding' Christ here, there and every-
where: in the city, in the poor, in the wilderness, in the rich
– according to taste! But, as Karl Barth once pointed out,
nowhere in the gospels are we told 'that the disciples sought
or found or even expected' the risen Christ.[2] Not that he

failed to come; his advent is recorded, again and again, but the initiative lies always with him: he 'drew near', he 'came' (as it were) from nowhere, he 'stood' on the seashore. His coming, in fact, is like that of a thief in the night or, as we might say, like a rare bird.

> It is when one is not looking,
> at times one is not there
>                     that it comes.

Hence the necessity of watchfulness, the need to 'wear the eyes out'.

Dr Edward Craig, of Churchill College, has epitomised the ethos of our modern Western culture as that of 'the agent in the void'.[3] That we are agents, responsible agents, the sole responsible agents around, we do not for one moment doubt. But within our energetic activism, our passion to make the world as we would have it be, there lies the terror that all this movement, this furious expenditure of intelligence and energy, is (as it were) a kind of thrashing around in formless dark or, perhaps, like the sea off the coast of Wales, a 'continuous waving that is without meaning'.

This, I think, is how it is, today as in the latter part of the nineteenth century, that presumption comes much closer to despair than might at first sight seem to be the case. Bursts of energy and bouts of listlessness, keeping on the move because the alternative might be extinction; there is no place (on either side of this) for patience, for stillness, for watchfulness – whether in our relationships with each other, or with natural objects, or with God.

> You must wear your eyes out.

Why? What on earth *for*? Notice that this question springs just as easily from despair as from presumption.

To track, with Aristotle, the path of virtue between contrasting vices does not imply (for instance) that hope is to be thought of as some kind of compromise or halfway house between presumption and despair. On the contrary, at least where faith, hope, and charity – the pattern of our relation to God – is concerned the contrasting vices resemble each other much more closely than they do the virtue to which they are opposed.

*The rare bird*

To the eyes of despair, we might say, the world is a nightmare; to the eyes of presumption, a daydream – castles in the air. But, light or dark, delightful or terrifying, a dream is a dream, and the dreamer stays asleep.

'Let us not fall asleep as others do, but let us keep awake and be sober' (5:6). In that passage, Paul sounds the keynote of our hope, the note which sounded to signal deliverance from Egypt and to call the exiles back from Babylon; the note which resonates in one of Bach's greatest chorales. 'Watch . . . lest he come suddenly and find you asleep' (Mark 13:35–36). What distinguishes Christians from other people (Karl Barth again) is 'that they have been awakened'.[4]

We ignore, at our peril, the irony in this, for few charges, these days, are more persistently and plausibly levelled against religious belief than that it functions as painkiller, narcotic, sleeping-pill, or (as the man said) 'opiate', dulling the pain of the dark and real world. And if we suppose this charge to be ill-founded, it will only be the evident quality of our watchfulness, our sustained and open-eyed alertness, which will show it to be so.

But, then, the question comes back again: what are we watching *for*? You will have noticed that R. S. Thomas seems almost to evade this question:

> Was I waiting for something?
> 　　　　Nothing
> but that continuous waving
> 　　that is without meaning
> occurred.

The point, surely, is that watching for God, waiting upon his coming, is not a matter of watching for any particular, predictable occurrence or kind of occurrence, because the mystery of God – upon whose saving presence we wait – is never to be identified with any particular fact, or dream, or image, or power, or occurrence, and especially not with the kind of dramatic occurrence, irruptive of the ordinary, which (in our childishness) we suppose to betoken the action of divinity. It is not so, and because it is not so, the presence of God is, as the poem goes on to say, for the most part indistinguishable by us from absence – which wears our eyes out.

But, we must keep awake, because he *does* come, *will* come, though the manner of his coming is that of the rare bird. And do not forget that there is no reason at all to suppose that the rare bird will be brightly plumaged, exotic, strikingly different from anything that we have ever seen before. On the contrary, it is just as likely that the rare bird will be small and brown and ordinary and inconspicuous, hidden in the reeds – like Moses in the bullrushes, or like almost any newborn Jewish child.

SELWYN COLLEGE, CAMBRIDGE,
29 NOVEMBER 1987

*Notes*

1. R. S. Thomas, 'Sea-Watching', *Laboratories of the Spirit* (London, 1975), p. 64.
2. Karl Barth, *Church Dogmatics* IV/2 (Edinburgh, 1958), p. 144.
3. See E. J. Craig, 'Philosophy and Philosophies', *Philosophy* vol. 58 (1983), pp. 189–201.
4. *Church Dogmatics* IV/2, p. 554.

# 5

# What is the world coming to?

Isaiah 33:13–22
Matthew 24:45—25:13

I have no personal experience of oppression. I have never
hungered and shivered, in some city subject to tyrannous
and alien rule, apprehensive of the soldiers, the police, the
strutting officials – all those whom Isaiah called the 'insolent people' (33:19) – who bark instructions or issue threats
in an 'obscure speech' which I 'cannot understand'.

The fact that I have no personal experience of these
things makes it that much more difficult for me accurately
to hear Isaiah's message. That passage cannot speak as
freshly, as directly, to me as it might to people whose circumstances were similar to those in which the message was originally uttered.

John Henry Newman often preached on this chapter of
Isaiah, and one of the ways in which he tried to meet the
difficulty was by shifting the images to more familiar contexts of darkness, constriction – and expectation:

> The very frost and cold, rain and gloom, which now befall
> us, forebode the last dreary days of the world, and in reli-
> gious hearts raise the thought of them . . . The season is
> chill and dark, and the breath of the morning is damp,
> and worshippers are few . . . Thus the soul is cast forward
> upon the future . . . [and], though the former things are
> failing; nay, rather . . . because they are failing, it will
> 'soon see the King in his beauty', and 'behold the land
> which is very far off'.[1]

Splendid stuff, but of course it simply won't do! The moderate discomforts of an Oxford November simply will not bear the weight of the misery and indignity addressed by Isaiah. If you transpose that kind of darkness, Isaiah's kind of darkness, into general metaphors of mortality, you correspondingly dilute the daylight with which Isaiah contrasts it.

I am not saying that it is impossible for people like us, in our Cambridge October, to 'hear' such a message, to be addressed by it. Clearly it is not. Inundated with newspaper reports and television images, we all have some second-hand sense of how things are – in Lebanon and Soweto, Afghanistan and Chile, perhaps even Belfast and Brixton – sufficient to give us some purchase on the context of the prophet's message.

We do have some sense of these things, albeit vicariously, and that is a start. But it is only a start. For knowledge of such suffering, whether at first or second hand, is not of itself sufficient to guarantee that we hear the message. We have next to consider: what kind of light is it that Isaiah's oracle throws into that kind of darkness?

Those marvellous images of the king in his beauty, of the far-stretched land, of the 'place of broad rivers and streams', fertile but not navigable by hostile navies, for there 'no galley with oars can go, nor stately ship can pass'; how are these pictures in fact brought to play upon the pain and darkness into which they are spoken?

There are some answers to this question which we can, I think, rule out from the start. Isaiah's images are certainly not reports or descriptions of future events. The future cannot be reported, because it has not yet happened.

It might help if we knew what kind of response the prophet expected from his hearers. In thus contrasting present domination with promised freedom, was he (for example) saying: 'Cheer up', or 'Hang on', or 'Stiffen your resistance'?

Having an appropriate respect for the experts, I consulted the commentaries on this – and got some rather dusty answers. According to one commentator, 'the poet's community' are being exhorted 'now to live in such a way that in the future they will have access to Zion and to their God'. But this doesn't answer my question. I want to know what kind of lifestyle, what practical pattern of enacted hope, is being required. I want to know what would count as 'such a way of living now'.

One reason why the commentaries do not answer these questions is that we do not know. We do not know enough about the particular circumstances of the text's production and therefore cannot tell how people in that darkness might appropriately have responded to the promise of light.

In fact, however, our ignorance, historically, as to the detailed facts of the case, matters less than we might suppose. 'The people who walked in darkness have seen a great light.' The question is: what are they supposed to do about it? – and that is not the kind of question which permits of abstract answers. 'Darkness', like 'desert', is a metaphor of deprivation, of imposed pain, resourcelessness, incapacity, provoking despair. But each pain is particular, sharply specific, edged and contoured. So also, therefore, are its remedies. When prophecy counteracts despair with the proclamation of hope, when it disturbs the darkness with promise of daylight, the hope engendered must, if it is not to be illusory, meet the requirements, match the contours, of the specific incapacity which it counteracts.

In other words, what is to count as hopeful behaviour, as watchfulness, as readiness to 'go out to meet the Bridegroom', is always a matter for practical judgement, for judgement arrived at by particular people in the light of particular circumstances. They may get it wrong, but they are surely more likely to get it right than those who issue abstract instructions (about resignation and non-violence, for example) from a safe distance.

One thing, at least, seems clear. As Isaiah brings his images of quietness and safety to play upon the unquiet circumstances of his threatened city, he is certainly not inviting his hearers to turn their attention away from the city, away from their present predicament, and to consider something else: say, the distant future. The pictures of the 'city of . . . appointed festivals', the 'quiet habitation', the 'tent' of

God's royal beauty, are not offered as palliatives or tranquil-
lisers, but as stimulants. His purpose is not distraction, but
the transmutation of lassitude into courage, of despair into
hope.

We are, in our culture, under strong pressure to suppose
otherwise, and thus to miss the message. Our society has
(often with our connivance) allocated a place to 'religion'
according to which the matter of our prayer, the content of
our contemplation, the message of the Scriptures, is taken
to be something other than the complex particular details
of mundane experience. We are under continual pressure
to dissociate spirit from flesh, gospel from culture, morality
from economics, religion from politics, eternity from time.
In the measure that we succumb to such pressure we
become incapable of achieving the kind of integration of
sensibility which would allow the prophetic word directly to
cast its disturbing light on all the ordinary things that we do
and undergo.

The brave man is not less brave because he quakes with
terror. Courage is a quality of action, not a feeling or an atti-
tude. And the same is true of hope (which is why, in the
Christian tradition, hope is said to be a virtue). Hope is not
a feeling, but a quality of action. And hope is not Christian
hope unless it is a quality of all our action, and all our suffering – mental and physical, domestic and economic, personal and political. This is why (or so it seems to me) the
achievement of what I have called the integration of sensibility is a necessary condition of hearing and responding to
the prophetic message.

What we require for this is a disciplining of our imagination, an informed purification of our sense and awareness
of what is actually happening – to us, and to other people.
If we misread the darkness, we shall misconceive the light.

Close your eyes, and wish the world were different, and
you cannot begin to hope. To be able to hope is to be awake,
to be watchful, to be awakened from sleep. Christian worship is not a pastime or an interlude from pain. It is, rather,
a pedagogy of watchfulness, a disciplining of attention, an

education in attentive reverence for God and for the features of his world.

But watchfulness is most subversive: it refuses to accept the self-estimation of the 'insolent people', of those whose counterfeit kingship it knows to be, not majesty, but fog – unstable darkness temporarily obscuring the appearance of 'the king in his beauty'. This, I think, is why one often finds, amongst those at the receiving end of the world's brutality, not merely dignity, but a kind of joy that is quite absent from the lamentations of those who wring their hands and wonder what the world is coming to. What *is* the world coming to? That is a secret – and it is a secret to which Isaiah, amongst others, knew the answer.

QUEENS' COLLEGE, CAMBRIDGE,
20 OCTOBER 1985

*Note*

1. John Henry Newman, *Parochial and Plain Sermons* 5 (London, 1868), pp. 1–2.

# 6

## Making things words

In this centenary year of the death of John Henry Newman,
I have often been reminded of the text which he took both
for the first sermon that he ever wrote and also for 'The
Parting of Friends', that poignant last sermon as an
Anglican before, in 1845, he became a Roman Catholic:
'Man goeth forth to his work and to his labour until the
evening.'

It comes, you remember, from Psalm 104, that most
magnificent of all the Bible's praises of creation. Creation is,
of course, God's work, from start to finish; God's still
unfinished and continuing, unending work; God's making
of a place in which his people live with him at peace. God's
work, God's making of a world, is not some distant, instant-
finished, magic moment: it is the whole sweep and labour,
darkness and daybreak, growth-pain and strenuous resolution, of the history of everything. And, in all this one great
and vastly varied work, each thing made has its own work to
do, its part to play, in the making of the whole:

> You set the earth on its foundations,
> . . .
> You cover it with the deep as with a garment;
> . . .
> At your rebuke [the waters] flee;
> At the sound of your thunder they take to flight.
> . . .
> You make springs gush forth in the valleys;
> they flow between the hills,
> giving drink to every wild animal;

. . .
By them the birds of the air have their habitation;
they sing among the branches.
. . .
You cause the grass to grow for the cattle,
and plants for people to cultivate,
to bring forth food from the earth,
and wine to gladden the human heart.
. . .
You have made the moon to mark the seasons;
the sun knows its time for setting.
You make darkness, and it is night,
when all the animals of the forest creep forth.
. . .
When the sun rises, they withdraw
and lie down in their dens.
Man goeth forth to his work
and to his labour until the evening.[1]

What kind of work is it, within this total scheme of things, that human beings have to do? What is specifically human work? A first clue as to the answer to this question is already given in the verses I have quoted. Human beings not only *find* their food, as other species do, but also *make* it, cultivate the soil, 'work up' the raw material of the world. And they do so, not simply in the interests of survival, bare necessity, but of community, of life together, common celebration – 'gladdened', perhaps, by wine!

To bring the sense of human work into somewhat sharper focus, I now propose to change the scene from rural Palestine to Moscow where, last January, I found myself one of a thousand delegates from more than eighty countries taking part in what was called the 'Global Forum on Environment and Development for Human Survival'. At different points in the vast hotel in which we stayed there were held, each morning, meditations – which explains why I was standing, before breakfast, in a circle of some fifty people at the centre of which a large ash tray was serving as a brazier. Round it there slowly circled an ancient Iroquois chief, intently murmuring. From time to time, he sprinkled tobacco on the fire (the Iroquois, I gather, have not yet discovered that tobacco is among the more ambiguous of God's gifts!).

They do, however, seem to have as highly developed a sense as did the ancient Hebrews of creation as ecosystem: of everything from thunderstorm to beetle, meadowland to nightfall, having its own particular and irreplaceable part to play in the rhythms and mechanisms of the working of the world. And *human* work, within this scheme of things? It falls to us, uniquely, to give thanks, to articulate creation's praise. Not only on our own behalf, but as the voice of every creature, we are the wordsmiths of the world and, as creation's poets, its priests. Hence the dawn-dance of an old man in the incongruous setting of a grey hotel close to Lenin's tomb.

There was a sadness in that song, for our generation can no longer innocently sing creation's praise. We are awakening to terrifying recognition of the fact that the ways in which we have 'worked up' the raw materials of the world are such as now to threaten the life chances not merely of our human children but of the very earth itself. We have made some of us thing-rich and all of us extremely poor. Our creation poems, our songs of praise, can only take the form of an acknowledgement of responsibility and a cry, from the heart of human emptiness, for our forgiveness and the world's redemption.

Wealth, in a healed world, would be a quality of existence rather than a quantity of things: the 'gladdened' company of other people in God's garden and before his face. And 'poverty', in such a world, would refer, not to loneliness and dispossession, but to that which makes each human being 'experience his greatest wealth – the *other* man – as need'.[2] And that, perhaps surprisingly, was a quotation from Karl Marx.

What Marx well understood, I think, were the terrifying costs of the processes whereby, under capitalism's Midas-touch, the abundant richness and vast diversity of things is drained away, homogenised, as everything becomes transformed into one only kind of thing: commodity. And, in this world, there are no longer values, only price; and where there once were endlessly diverse responsibilities and relationships, now there are only relationships of production, distribution and exchange. The jargon name for this strange alchemy is 'universalisation of the commodity form'. And, as its chill, grey blanket rolls across the world, transmuting all the natural elements into one (not gold, in fact, nor even paper now, but figures flickering on computer screens) people grow lonely and afraid.

'We live', said Václav Havel, President of Czechoslovakia, in his Inaugural Address,

> in a contaminated moral environment . . . We learnt not to believe in anything, to ignore each other, to care only about ourselves. Concepts such as love, friendship, compassion, humility or forgiveness lost their depth and dimensions and for many of us represented only psychological peculiarities, or they resembled gone-astray greetings from ancient times, a little ridiculous in the era of computers and spaceships.[3]

And one unforeseen effect of the crumbling of communist collectivism has been to highlight the poverty and moral impotence of Western individualism which, as Michael Ignatieff put it in the *Observer* earlier this year, has rendered us 'incoherent about why we should care about the political welfare of [other] individuals when our own interests are not at stake'.

We have before us now two models of the working of the world, and of our place within it. On the one hand, the nightmare mechanisms of a global supermarket – bright-packaged, ephemeral, destructive, morally vacuous and devoid of meaning – operated and inhabited by lonely and exhausted individuals (and they are the lucky ones – the rest are left outside). On the other hand, the nostalgic daydream of a world of pastoral harmony, birdsong and eco-bliss.

But dreams and nightmares are just that: they are not direct descriptions of the actual state of things. The psalmist is not describing the Palestine of his day – which was, we may presume, a place of drought and warfare, disease and sudden death. His vision is of a world as it would be if healed, redeemed, brought into harmony with the Creator's will. It is a vision of hope, which points the way in which things may be helped to go.

Similarly with the nightmare of 'Great Britain PLC'. Even a government hell-bent on fostering the omnivorous proclivities of the commodity form could never quite succeed in reducing all of us and everything to price tags. The nightmare warns us how things go in the measure that capitalism is unchecked and uncorrected by other visions, other considerations, other estimations of the way the world is and of our part in it.

It was, I think, the Iroquois chief who gave us the clue as to where the necessary corrective resources might be sought. He reminded us that human work – work both appropriate to our species' 'niche' within the total scheme of things and, as such, enhancing our humanity – is *word*work. We are, I said, the wordsmiths of the world.

We quite misunderstand this message, however, if we take it to mean that human work is a matter of 'mere' words, not deeds, of hot air rather than hard work. To say that it is our task, through the ways in which we 'work up' the raw materials of the world, to give things voice and render praise to God, is to say that we are called to be craftsmen bringing out the shape and form and meaning of the world. All poets are craftsmen, engineers; and engineering, we might say, is 'concrete poetry'.

There are, in fact, no 'mere' words, just as there are no human deeds devoid of meaning. Deeds well done are eloquent – hence the proverbial recognition that 'actions speak louder than [mere] words'. And, on the other hand, good words, strong and serious words, words like 'I promise' or 'I love you', make all the difference in the world. They change the world. In fact, they *make* the world. 'In the beginning was the Word.' And God said: 'Let there be light.'

The Scriptures portray God's work, his work of worldmaking, as utterance, declaration of love, and promise;

utterance that goes from the very heart of God all the way to Calvary. Our task, within this work of God – a task at once religious, political, economic, industrial and educational – is the endless labour of learning to rediscover and respect the difference and dignity and identity and significance of things, thus transforming 'mere' objects into symbols, dead matter into living speech, commodities into gifts. Our task, within the creative work of God, is that of finding and fashioning, within the world, a home.

'Man goeth forth unto his work and to his labour until the evening.' But, Newman added, 'evening falls before [the work] is done.' No matter; we are only called to do whatever we can do in our place in the daylight time allowed to us. The rest is in God's hands, strong hands, safe hands, which will come to rest only when his whole work is done.

PREACHED AT THE ANNUAL SERVICE OF THE LONDON INDUSTRIAL CHAPLAINCY, 21 MAY 1990

*Notes*

1. I have left this last verse (verse 23) in the form in which Newman knew and used it. The NRSV has: 'People go out to their work and to their labour until the evening.'
2. Karl Marx, *Early Writings* (London, 1975), p. 356.
3. Vaclav Havel, *Open Letters: Selected Prose 1965–1990*, ed. Paul Wilson (London, 1991), p. 391.

# 7

## The valley of bones

Ezekiel 37:1–14
Romans 6:3–9
Luke 23:44—24:6

'They say, "Our bones are dried up, and our hope is lost; we are completely cut off"' (37:11).

The second Letter to Timothy tells us, quite firmly, that 'All scripture is inspired by God and useful for teaching . . . and for training in righteousness' (2 Timothy 3:16). Very true, and very important. Nevertheless, most of us, I think, especially as we grow older, find that particular parts of the Scriptures come to occupy a special place in our thinking and praying. Like old ships, covered with barnacles, these special passages become encrusted with memories. Because of what we have learnt, or laughed, or suffered, in their company, they come (as it were) to focus the whole message of the Gospel for our experience and understanding of it. (In my own case, I know that if, shipwrecked on a desert island, I were allowed only two passages of Scripture, they would be the Prologue to the Fourth Gospel and the story, in Luke, of the journey to Emmaus.)

I was in Boston last week when I heard the news of Father David's death, and also learnt that he had asked that I should preach at this Mass. On thing, at least, was immediately clear to me: the first reading would have to come from the book of Ezekiel. It was, quite definitely, David's desert island book.

The only thing I was not sure about was whether the reading should be the great charge, in chapter 34, against the self-serving shepherds of Israel (in place of whom God promises a *good* shepherd to lead his people home), or whether it should be the vision of the valley of dry bones. I decided, after some reflection, to choose the valley of dry bones because that would concentrate our minds on what it was that David tried to *do* – whereas the consideration of the qualities of a pastor would have put the spotlight more directly onto *him*: which he most certainly would not want.

All this pondering was, of course, a waste of time. David himself had things well under control: almost the first thing I learnt on returning to England on Saturday was that he had specified, in writing, that the first reading at this Mass should be the one to which we listened just now. (But at least my instinct had been sound!)

'Our bones are dried up, and our hope is lost; we are cut off completely.' The people of God are in exile, cut off from home, cut off from Jerusalem. There is some evidence that, before they were taken into captivity, the prophet Ezekiel was there, in Palestine, a witness to that last losing struggle. The valley of dry bones is a deserted battlefield.

Even warfare has energy and a kind of life. But it is difficult to imagine a more dead place, a place from which the spirit has been more completely extinguished, than a desert battlefield strewn with bodies so long dead that the vultures have picked the skeletons clean: 'our bones are dried up'.

This, then, is what the Jews felt like, in exile in Babylon, and it is against this bleak landscape of despair that the prophet sees God's promise breathing life back, making again a people, an army, to be taken home.

The word for breath, or wind, or spirit, here, is the same word as that used in the book of Genesis, in the making of humankind: 'God formed man from the dust of the ground, and breathed into his nostrils the breath of life; and the man became a living being' (Genesis 2:7). And now, in this dead valley, God breathes again, Adam is made again; men and women walk again.

Sometimes, in the Bible, God is thought of as a rock, a stronghold, a place of shelter, somewhere to run to. But,

very often, God's presence and activity, his life-giving spirit,
has all the disconcerting and disruptive power, the unpre-
dictability, of wind and storm. God's breath gives life, and
vitality is no tame toy.

David Woodard knew full well the importance of stability,
of stillness, of finding and furnishing fixed points. But, tem-
peramentally, his formidable energies tended in the other
direction. Given the context and the cause, he was a stirrer
and shaker (bones could rattle a bit when he was around!).

But temperament was only part of the story. He knew that
these were times in which it was of paramount importance
for the Church to stir itself, to wake from sleep, to stop confusing custom with tradition, to flex long unused muscles in
response to the call of the Gospel and the needs of God's
people.

(The range of his interests helped him here. He was, for
example, a voracious reader. I live among some of the best-
stocked libraries and bookshops in the world, but it was in
the presbytery here, at Oundle, last summer, that I first saw
a copy of Professor Copleston's new study of Russian philosophy.)

'They say, "Our bones are dried up, and our hope is lost;
we are cut off completely". Therefore prophesy, and say to
them, Thus says the Lord God: "I will put my spirit within
you, and you shall live, and I will place you on your own
soil"' (37:11, 14). It is, I suppose, impossible for us – as
Christians, as Easter people, as people whose faith is
focused on the promise of resurrection begun in Jesus – not
to hear echoes of that hope in Ezekiel's prophecy.

Nevertheless, it is, I think, important to remember that
neither Ezekiel, nor his contemporaries, believed in a general resurrection of the dead. What Ezekiel is saying is that
a people which seems to be 'dead', as a people – vanquished
and far from home, will be brought back to life, as a people;
will be brought home again to Palestine. 'I am going to
open your graves . . . my people; and I will bring you back
to the land of Israel' (37:13).

The hope held out by the vision of the valley of dry bones
is, in other words, a quite down-to-earth practical and polit-

ical hope: a hope of release from oppression and return from exile. And the reason why it is important for *us* to remember this is that our Easter hope is hollow and unreal unless it takes flesh, finds form, in the day-to-day business of practical politics, of 'people-making'.

The best way to find out whether people really believe in the life-giving, flesh-finding, spirit of the risen Christ is to see what they do about the homeless and the poor, about those exiled from warmth, and comfort, and security. Perhaps, in England these days, we need two kinds of prophesying: the voice of Ezekiel to bring hope to the poor, and the voice of Amos to denounce the destructive hypocrisies of the rich.

'Our bones are dried up, and our hope is lost.' Their hope was lost because Jerusalem had fallen, and the Jews had looked on Jerusalem as the indestructible guarantee of their survival. When the supposedly indestructible city was destroyed, their hope went with it. Cities, possessions, certainties, prejudices: the list of things to which we desperately cling, as tokens of *our* indestructibility, is endless. And when these things *are* destroyed, when they are taken from us, then (too often) our hope goes with them.

I have known few people who learnt, quite as impressively as Father David did, how to travel light. He was, in the proper sense, a most unworldly man; that is to say: he loved good sights and sounds (not least the lute), good food and drink, ideas and company; but he loved them as gifts, not as possessions to be clung to like a child's comforter.

But when I say he learnt to travel light, I do not mean that he 'held lightly' the central certainties and moral imperatives of our faith. On the contrary, he learnt to distinguish essentials from non-essentials, the things that really mattered from those that mattered less or not at all. And this, I think, was the secret of his passion for Christian unity, of which the shared church of St Andrew's, Cippenham, is so impressive an expression. (Although I've heard it told of other places, I still think that it was the Anglican priest at Cippenham who first thought up that slogan for the tabernacle at St Andrew's: 'In case of unity, break glass!') It is evident how deeply David would have appreciated the generosity of the Anglican parish here, in Oundle, in offering us their church today for this Mass.

'I prophesied as he commanded me, and the breath came into them, and they lived' (37:10). During the more than thirty years of his priestly ministry, he helped the breath back, renewed the hope, in very many people. The often awkward shyness which sheltered his gentleness meant, I think, that he found it far more difficult to receive than to give affection. But no one who knew him could doubt his capacity for feeling – and hence his vulnerability. I know how much the long estrangement from his father meant to him, *and* how much its healing.

'Our bones are dried up, and our hope is lost.' Not so! David Woodard lived the denial of that despair with passion. And this Eucharist which we celebrate today, in gratitude for his life and ministry, we celebrate with him in the certainty that God's Spirit will breathe flesh onto all our bones, and bring us home.

PREACHED AT THE REQUIEM MASS FOR DAVID WOODARD,
OUNDLE, 21 MARCH 1988

# ATTENTIVENESS

# 8

## Enquiry and attentiveness

Luke 2:41–51

The Reverend John Hulse, who died on the fourteenth of December, 1790, at the age of eighty-two, devoted a large part of his life to composing and amending his will. The body of the text of what his memorialist called 'this extraordinary document' runs to nearly four hundred pages of closely written manuscript, to which are appended nine codicils. Not that I am in any position to criticise Mr Hulse's testatory obsession, standing, as I do, doubly indebted to his benefaction.

In one section of the will, the Hulsean Preacher's duties are spelt out with great clarity and in considerable detail. While it is my business 'to demonstrate in the most convincing manner the truth and excellence of Christianity', I am forbidden to descend 'to any particular sects or controversies . . . amongst Christians themselves, except some new or dangerous error either of superstition or enthusiasm, as of Popery or Methodism . . . should prevail'. In view of this stipulation, and notwithstanding the fact that both Methodism and Popery seem to be in quite good health throughout the university, I shall not descend to their consideration.

30 November 1892. On that date, almost exactly at the mid-point between today and John Hulse's death, died one of Cambridge's most distinguished theologians, F. J. A. Hort. In his Hulsean Lectures (delivered in 1871) Dr Hort said this: 'the new worlds conquered for knowledge give promise to aid powerfully in bringing the unity of all truth

in Him who said "I am the truth", and thus in raising knowledge of truth to the place which He marked out for it in the
gathering of man to God.'

The dominant ethos or climate of belief, today, is different from both Hulse's robust apologetic instinct and Hort's
vision of the gathering into unity of truth. Yet, in the duty
that faith owes to our human quest for understanding, we
can find common threads, continuing concerns. In particular, there are deep and intimate connections between that
prayerfulness or disciplined attention which is the heart of
Christian faith and the passionate disinterestedness, attentiveness to truth, on which the flourishing of a university
depends.

The media have recently displayed much interest in reviv-
ing the debate between C. P. Snow's 'two cultures'. This
great divide between two worlds – one labelled 'science' and
the other 'arts' – was always quite unreal. The only way to
make it plausible is to suppose that universities are popu-
lated, more or less exclusively, by white-coated physicists of
terrifying mathematical intelligence, on the one hand, and,
on the other, by absent-minded cricket-loving persons issu-
ing obscure editions of Euripides.

But if some visitor from outer space were to wander, innocently but observantly, around the university today, it would,
I think, be struck by two things. The first would be the exu-
berant and irreducible diversity of all the different kinds of
things we do. Glance through the lecture list and notice that
we work at local government finance and molecular biol-
ogy; radio astronomy and Chinese grammar; psychoanalysis
and the archaeology of ancient Egypt; insurance law and
heart disease; Aristotle's ethics and computer-aided archi-
tectural design; quantum mechanics and the sociology of
education. There simply is no way in which this wealth of
enterprises, skills, techniques and habits of enquiry, this
throng of methods, arguments and practices, can be rallied
round two and only two imperial banners extravagantly
labelled 'art' and 'science'. We do many different things,
and most of us have only hazy, second-hand and ill-

informed ideas of what the rest of us are up to. That first thing that our visitor would see.

But the second is that there *is* a common thread which binds us all together. Increasingly, it seems to me, every department, each small area of particular expertise, is gripped by paranoia. We each know that the things we do and care about are underfunded, under threat, insufficiently appreciated and most misunderstood.

This climate of demoralised distrust, exacerbated by funding strategies which view markets as scenes of cut-throat competition rather than exchange, corrodes that strenuous and endlessly demanding common quest for understanding which is the heartbeat of a university.

All this is easily and often said. And it is, by now, common-place to point out how paradoxical it is that we should be strengthening the forces of fragmentation at the very moment when – from physics to philosophy, from econom-ics to ecology – it is on all sides freshly recognised that we are one people forming one small world: that all our lives, our enterprises, and indeed our destiny, are woven together in one single, fragile web. We may not say, as easily as Hort did, that our new knowledge *promises* to aid in 'bringing in the unity of all truth in Him who said "I am the truth"', but that new knowledge does seem daily to render the recogni-tion of our *duty* to that unity imperative.

This does not mean that we can suddenly see all things whole, or making single sense, because we cannot. But that is no excuse for setting limits to attentiveness. We can still say, with Newman: 'I would open my heart, if not my intel-lect (for that is beyond me), to the whole circle of truth.'[1] Education in contemplativity is, at least in part, education in opening the heart, in disciplined attentiveness, in watchful, not uncritical, receptiveness to unfamiliar truth.

Research and scholarship require, in any field, a passion-ate disinterestedness, a consuming dedication patiently to try to learn, that is not simply similar to faith's obedience to the mystery of God but, on a Christian reading, is an aspect of its very form. The opening of our heart to truth, which may be for the most part most mundane and (as it seems)

quite fruitless labour, is, or at least may be, on faith's reading of the world as God's creation, a form of prayer.

Unfaith, the closure of the heart, resistance to God's
truth, is spoken of in Scripture, metaphorically, as failure
both to 'hear' and 'see'. Though we may conjure up visions
and make a lot of noise, we dread the darkness, the
unspeaking emptiness, that seems to lie behind them. Faith,
on the other hand, is a kind of seeing in the dark, a listening to stillness.

In Western culture, especially in modern times, we speak
of understanding and the quest for knowledge primarily in)
terms of 'sight'. So much so, indeed, that we no longer
notice that, when we say we 'see' this, that, or the other,
what, in fact, we usually mean is that we have 'seen the
point', that something has been understood. Thus, even
though you are, at present, listening to me, I might well ask
you whether or not you 'see' what I am getting at.

There is, however, an important difference between sight
and hearing. We turn our heads from left to right, alter our
vision. In looking at the world, observing things around us,
there is a sense in which we take the initiative, keep in control, decide just what to see. We hear things, on the other
hand, from all around us. Moreover, whatever lies within
our field of vision we can see. Even good camouflage does
not make things invisible. But we only hear things if they
make a sound. If they stay silent, there is nothing that (as
hearers) we can do about it.

In our consideration of the ways in which we grow in
knowledge, deepen understanding, the language of 'hearing' or 'attentiveness' thus highlights, in a way that talk of
'seeing' does not, the extent to which we are not masters of
the world, centres of existence. We only hear when someone speaks. It is responsiveness which brings us to the truth.
Faith may be, indeed, a way of seeing in the dark but, in all
its forms, faith comes by hearing.

I am, in other words, suggesting that the language of
'hearing' or 'attentiveness' brings out, as talk of 'seeing'
does not, the way in which all understanding, all growth in
knowledge, presupposes trust. Not gullibility – adult trust,

like all mature relationship, is only slowly and quite painfully grown into with experience. And yet, without the kind of courage risking vulnerability, without reliance on each other, on the evidence as tested, on the procedures we employ, on a million unnoticed features of the familiar world, nothing whatsoever gets discovered, thought out, done.

'His mother', says the gospel that we heard, 'treasured all these things in her heart' (2:51). One paradigm of Christian attentiveness is Mary's faith, responsive to God's Word. She is described by St Augustine, in a sermon preached to catechumens, as 'conceiving Christ in her mind before doing so in her womb'. Or, as he put it, more succinctly, in the same sermon: 'By believing, she conceived him whom she bore for our belief.' Through Mary's hearing, God's Word speaks in time and place. In her attentiveness, God's Word takes flesh.

And yet, the most extraordinary thing about that passage in Luke's gospel is its description of the form that fleshed Word takes: 'they found him . . . sitting among the teachers, listening to them and asking them questions' (2:46). I said earlier that it is responsiveness which brings us to the truth. This principle could hardly find more paradoxical, more subversive expression than in the suggestion that it is God's own responsiveness which brings us to his truth; that attentiveness, enquiry, questions to the teachers, are an aspect of God's Word's utterance in the world.

We celebrate the liturgy, take part in services, say prayers, from time to time. But such explicit, ritualised attentiveness should be the distillation of that uninterrupted prayerfulness, continual contemplativity, which is our life, as Christians: life lived, in faith, before the mystery of God.

Contemplation as the life of faith and praying is – like thinking or like loving – entirely natural, spontaneous, uninterruptible, and desperately difficult to do well. No one needs a PhD to think, or love – or pray, yet none of us, however hard we work at it, will ever adequately or appropriately pray – or love, or think. Civilisation, culture, life in the Spirit – call it what you will – is unending schooling, never-finished discipline, in patterns of appropriate attentiveness: in love, and thought, and prayer.

And if, as I suggested earlier, the culture of the university is threatened by self-doubt, suspicious fragmentation, structures of competitiveness inimical to the discovery of some sense of how things hang together, then perhaps we might best 'demonstrate . . . the truth and excellence of Christianity', in a modern university, by fostering counter-cultures of attentiveness contributing, however indirectly, to the 'gathering of humankind to God'.

HULSEAN SERMON
PREACHED BEFORE THE UNIVERSITY OF CAMBRIDGE,
28 FEBRUARY 1993

*Note*

1. John Henry Newman, *The Idea of a University*, ed. I. T. Ker (Oxford, 1976), p. 456.

# 9

## St Valentine, women and love

Genesis 29:1–20
John 4:1–15

The newspapers bear witness, on this feast of Valentine, to the inventiveness of unconstrained imagination. St Valentine need not detain us long, because the historians are not even able to decide whether there were one of them or two, what happened to him or them, or where it happened. (They all, however, seem agreed that he, or they, came to a most unpleasant end.)

It is, I am told, the *date* that matters more: this mid-February day whose association with courtship has some connection with the pagan feast of Lupercalia. In case some of you have forgotten the details of this celebration, let me refresh your memory, with the help of the *Oxford Classical Dictionary*:

> After the sacrifice of a goat or goats and a dog . . . at the Lupercal, a cave below the western corner of the Palatine, youths, naked except for girdles made from the skins of the victims, ran about the bounds of the Palatine settlement, striking those whom they met, especially women, with strips of the goat-skins.

This may not seem, so far, to be promising material for a sermon on love. Nor does the situation greatly improve when we go on to read that this 'whole ceremony reflects the needs of a small pastoral community'. I wonder what the late John Arlott would have made of this view of village life!

Pastoral life in ancient Rome (with or without the goings-on at the western corner of the Palatine) is quite alien to our experience. And yet it is no further from us, culturally, than pastoral life in ancient Palestine. We are, however, always tempted to short-cut this and too quickly to try to take the shepherd tribes of Israel as our familiars and contemporaries.

'So Jacob served seven years for Rachel, and they seemed to him but a few days because of the love he had for her' (29:20). 'In the light of words like these' (comments the *Interpreter's Bible*) 'Jacob's remoteness in time and place passes like a shadow, and he is at one with all lovers of every age in the timeless wonder of the meeting of man and maid.'

Jacob's 'remoteness', the genuine difference between his time and ours, which makes the effort of interpreting the text both hard work and worthwhile, is thus brushed aside as 'shadow'. In its place, however, we are given nothing more substantial than the pastel shades of sentimentality – the illusion that love takes people out of time.

To take love out of time, however, is also to take it from the *body*, for bodies are distinctly temporal things – inexorable processes of birth and growth, decay and mortality. 'The timeless wonder of the meeting of man and maid.' A far cry, certainly, from running naked round the hills of Rome, beating the girls with bits of goatskin, but (perhaps) uncomfortably close to Mills and Boon.

There is a hint of this earlier in the same commentary. Jacob suggests to the shepherds that, since 'it is still broad daylight, it is not time for the animals to be gathered together; water the sheep, and go, pasture them'; to which the shepherds reply: 'We cannot until all the flocks are gathered together, and the stone is rolled from the mouth of the well; then we water the sheep.' Two verses later, as Rachel approaches with Laban's sheep, 'Jacob went up and rolled the stone from the well's mouth, and watered the flock of Laban' (29:7–8, 10).

The text, as we have it, bristles with inconsistency, not least because it is a patchwork woven from different traditions concerning the history of relationships between various tribes and places and peoples. But from this process there was produced a text, a tale, as we now have it, and it is surely in order to take it so. And, when we do, we notice, in verse 8, that the shepherds do not roll away the stone while, in verse 10, Jacob, on sight of Rachel, does so single-handed. 'In contact with Rachel', says the commentary, 'Jacob from the first moment was a different man.' But, wait a minute! The story does not say that Jacob *could* not move the stone before; it only indicates the reason which the other shepherds gave for having not yet done so. 'Jacob from the first moment was a different man.' Surely this transformation from wimp to Superman in the twinkling of a maiden's eye owes more to the interpreter's notion of 'true love' than to such evidence as the text affords?

There is, I am suggesting, some kind of connection between abstract sentimentality and the failure seriously to engage in the labour of interpretation. Both are forms of self-indulgence, of egotism, of the failure to take care. But taking care takes time, attentiveness takes time, because speaking takes time. And speaking takes time because it is flesh-speech, body language. The angels may not need time, but we do.

What makes human animals different from other animals is that their bodies speak, their actions signify. Lust, we might say, is inhuman because it is un-languaged love, carnality careless of its utterance.

It is often said that nervousness of the carnal character of human loving arises from fear of the flesh. It seems to me more plausible to suggest that it is rooted in egotism: in terror of the *messages* of the flesh, of what might actually be asked of us if we risked opening our hearts to the pleas of other people, people different from ourselves, disruptive of our tranquil certainties and not amenable to our control. (Hence the close kinship between puritanism and pornography.)

Here are some lines from a sonnet by George Herbert on 'Love'. As I read them, keep in mind my suggestion that lust is unlanguaged love:

Immortall Heat, O let thy greater flame
    Attract the lesser to it: let those fires,
Which shall consume the world, first make it tame;
And kindle in our hearts such true desires,
As may consume our lusts, and make thee way.
    Then shall our hearts pant thee; then shall our brain
    All her invention on thine Altar lay . . .

We sometimes suppose that the thing to do with lust is to douse it: 'Take a cold shower' – fire-engine philosophy. George Herbert, however, prays that God 'consume our lusts' not by quenching passion, stifling desire, but by inflaming it: 'kindle in our hearts such true desires.' And true desire, on this account, is desire antithetical to egotism. It beats with the rhythm of the other's need – 'then shall our hearts pant thee'; and all its ingenuity and labour is set at the service of the beloved: 'then shall our brain/All her invention on thine Altar lay.'

Love out of time is fantasy, illusion, self-indulgence. Love takes time (as Jacob knew, who served seven years for Rachel – even if, because of the love he had for her, time flew!). Love takes time, needs painstaking practical attentiveness to the other's needs. And attentiveness is a matter of interpretation, of decoding the message of another's flesh.

I said just now that what makes human animals different is that their bodies speak. But this, of course, was not quite true, was only half the story. It is not communication, message-sending, as such, which makes us different, but our ability to remember and make plans. Our flesh has language which goes far beyond the instant of its utterance. It's this great freight, of memory and prospect, which human language bears, that gives our loving such frightening risk and boundless possibility.

There is a line of Auden's which makes the point beautifully:

    'Words are for those with promises to keep.'[1]

Human beings are the product of other people's promises, and their sufferings, in no small measure, are the consequences of betrayal, of promises unkept. Now our turn comes: we cannot fail to speak, in all our actions, and every expression of attraction, interest or desire, carries – in code – its consequences.

Official Christianity has a most uneven record in its treatment of sexuality: a record too much compounded of puritanism purporting to be purity; of fear of the feminine masquerading as the love of God. But, when all this has been said, it also must be said that there is something disturbingly unreal about the image (beloved by those who suppose themselves superior to all taboos) of sex as 'good clean fun'.

However laudable (in view of our urgent need to come to grips with a disease of quite appalling deadliness) the motives of those who urge 'safe sex' upon us, it must be tirelessly insisted that, for us humans, sex has never been nor ever can be 'safe'.

'Words are for those with promises to keep.' Sex is dangerous because you and I are unreliable; because we enter (beyond the possibility of adequate calculation) into commitments we have neither the strength nor the generosity to sustain. Sex is also dangerous because, unique of all the animals, our love is languaged, bears promises – promises at whose heart (subverting the warm world our ego sleeps in) there lies the exhilarating possibility of transformative, liberating friendship.

All human loving speaks, simultaneously, of heaven and of hell, of undying friendship and irreversible betrayal. Our loving makes us nervous (or should do so) because the evidence shows all too clearly the fragility of solidarity and the dark consequences of unfaithfulness.

And yet, neither the first word nor the last are ours. 'Words are for those with promises to keep.' And all things happen, all chains of consequence fall out, in ultimate dependence on the fidelity of that one Word which makes and heals the world.

The first word is with God. So also is the last. He keeps his promise. Hope is sustainable through darkness and through tragedy because of that conviction. 'Our hearts *pant* thee.'

Love, all our loving – for each other, for ourselves, for fruit
and flowers, fraternity and freedom, and for God – is a form
of *thirst*. A thirst that seems unquenchable: as Jesus said, at
Jacob's well, 'Every one who drinks of this water will be
thirsty again' (4:13).

Love takes time (usually much more than seven years).
But the time it takes, and the burden of risk that it bears, are
made supportable, made *joyfully* supportable, by the knowledge that we are already washed by the bright spring
flowing from that well, that watering-place whose stone was
moved, at Easter, not by Jacob's effort, but by the passionate
fidelity, the heartflame, of God's love.

PETERHOUSE, CAMBRIDGE,
14 FEBRUARY 1993

*Note*

1. The last line of 'Their Lonely Betters', written in 1950.

# LIGHT

# 10

## Prophecy and clarity

In September 1940, Dietrich Bonhoeffer drafted the opening pages of that section of his *Ethics* which is entitled 'Ethics as Formation'. 'Today', he wrote,

> there are once more villains and saints, and they are not hidden from the public view. Instead of the uniform greyness of the rainy day we now have the black storm-cloud and the brilliant lightning flash. The outlines stand out with exaggerated sharpness. Reality lays itself bare. Shakespeare's characters walk in our midst.[1]

It is, perhaps, Iago rather than Henry V that he had in mind.

'Reality lays itself bare.' But to whom did it seem to do so? In a recent issue of *The Tablet*, John Harriott reflected on the matter-of-fact presentation, in the film *Shoah*, of the ordinary person's complicity in the Holocaust. For Harriott, the film's most striking lesson was 'the commonplace character of evil, the ordinariness of the wicked. A relatively few fanatical ideologues', he wrote, 'were able to commit this most appalling crime because many times their number . . . doctors, bureaucrats, university professors, businessmen', found excuses 'to carry on regardless as if their powers of moral discrimination had been put to sleep'.[2]

For most people, for the sleepwalkers, reality did *not* 'lay itself bare'. They had no vision of Shakespeare's characters. All they seem to have seen was, indeed, 'the uniform greyness of the rainy day'. And the consequences of this clouding of the moral imagination were catastrophic.

This would not, I think, have surprised Bonhoeffer. The

passage that I quoted is followed by an extended analysis of moral moods and attitudes, sustained with good reason, and from the best of intentions, which nevertheless inhibit us from seeing what lies before our eyes and acting accordingly.

Thus, for example, he says that he is 'distressed by the failure of *reasonable* people to perceive either the depths of evil or the depths of the holy'. Reasonable people are 'so blind that in their desire to see justice done to both sides they are crushed between the two clashing forces and end by achieving nothing'.[3]

A second example is provided by those who suppose that 'the way out from the confusing multiplicity of possible decisions is the path of duty.' Following that path, and knowing ourselves to be bewildered and mesmerised by 'the uniform greyness of the rainy day', we suppose the responsibility for clear-sightedness to lie elsewhere, to be shouldered by our superiors. 'The man of duty', says Bonhoeffer, 'will end by having to fulfil his obligation even to the devil.'[4]

For us, forty years later, with the images of Nuremberg and the trial of Eichmann in our memory, that particular pattern of self-deception, that particular narcotic to our powers of moral discrimination, is likely, I think, to take a somewhat different and perhaps more subtle form. It is not now our 'social superiors', in Church or State, to whom, in the name of duty, we pass the burden of responsibility for clear-sightedness. It is, rather, the 'experts', unnamed and omniscient, to whom (we are told, again and again) we must now bend the knee, defer all judgement as to what is actually happening and, therefore, as to what may appropriately be done.

And so, rendered indecisive by our reasonableness and our acknowledged ignorance of detailed fact, we carry on regardless as if our powers of moral discrimination had been put to sleep.

'Reality lays itself bare.' There are, it seems to me, three areas in which it is only the clouding of our moral imagination by reasonableness and misplaced deference to expertise that prevents us from seeing, in the lightning flash, Iago walking in our midst.

(Iago, by the way, is not an individual. There is little evidence that Bonhoeffer had primarily Adolf Hitler in mind. Iago is a symbol, a dramatisation of forces and structures of destructiveness.)

The three areas that I have in mind are, firstly, the failure of policies of deterrence, as actually intended and executed, to diminish the danger of nuclear war; secondly, the cumulative effect of economic, financial and political policy in Europe and the United States on the countries of the 'South', of the Third World; and, thirdly, the mounting evidence of the alienation, destitution and social instability that is the actual though unintended consequence of policy within our own country.

In all three areas, reality only fails to 'lay itself bare' because complex and theoretically justifiable patterns of self-deception are putting to sleep our powers of moral discrimination. At every level, from the family to the nation and the alliance of nations, human groups tend to act in their own interest. But the energy with which those interests are pursued sometimes springs from the conviction that they are, in fact, the interests of humanity itself. One fundamental form of self-deception is self-interest disguised as altruism. Egotism walking in its sleep.

Thus, for example, in East–West relations, we identify the defence of the West with the defence of human freedom, the freedom of all mankind. To our clouded vision, 'our' enemy appears to be the enemy of the human race. East and West mistrust each other, supposing mistrust to be justified because the 'other side' are untrustworthy. What both sides fail to notice is that the 'other' is untrustworthy because he cannot be relied upon to share the identification of our side's interests with the interests of humankind.

Pursuing our own particular interests under the illusion that they are the interests of humankind, it does not occur to us that the projects and policies that we endorse could be darkly destructive. We gaze at sickening images of strife and starvation. Our compassion is aroused, but not our guilt.

This is not *our* doing because we know ourselves to be, at worst, bystanders and, at best, benefactors of mankind.

And so, when famine sweeps the Sahara, we attribute it to 'natural disaster' or the profligacy of African governments; we weep a little, and 'carry on regardless'. World trade is a very complicated business, best left to the experts. No point in peering through the drizzle. The greyness is preferable to the lightning flash that would lay bare the reality of our active contribution to the deaths of a million children.

Nearer to home, as the social fabric creaks and inner-city destitution spreads like dry rot, we know that whoever or whatever is responsible it cannot be us: it must be some combination of inexorable market forces and other people's wickedness. How could it be 'us'? 'We' have only the nation's interests at heart, in the defence of which, accordingly, we strengthen the forces of law and order.

In these and countless other ways we deceive ourselves through the prosecution of self-interest disguised as altruism. And, in all this, there is a subtle idolatry at work. The trouble with idolatry, of course, is that it does not simply mistake the identity of God but destroys human beings in the process. If we were awake, there would be no feature of the world that we would worship. Sleep-walking, we worship the abstractions that populate our dreaming. In the name of 'freedom', we sustain tyranny; in the name of 'order', we systematise disorders that we do not heal but merely hide from view.

All this, of course, is banal and familiar, because we find it only too easy to discern other people's idolatry. But it is *self*-deception, as the fundamental form of evil's ordinariness, on which I am inviting us to meditate.

The 'reality' is the clash of countless competing egotisms, some trivial, some almost uncontrollably powerful. Reality fails to 'lay itself bare' because our egotism, whoever 'we' are, remains largely invisible. We think we see Iago walking over there, and fail to notice his feet fitting our footsteps.

Who, or what, might wake us up, might open our eyes, dissipate the mists of self-deception, enable us to see with clarity the facts before us? Well, let us imagine that there were some group or movement which, while sharing the language and memory, sorrow and joy, poetry, landscape and tragedy of its own particular place and people, yet knew itself to share their guilt, their egotism, destructiveness and propensity towards idolatry.

The 'clear-sightedness' of such a group would spring from its refusal to invest particular interest with universal significance, its refusal idolatrously to ascribe absolute value to any particular institution, tradition, ambition or idea. This refusal would not be an expression of cynicism, or of the illusion that its hands were clean, but rather of the passionate conviction that, ultimately, we have nothing to fear but the dream-world of self-deception, the destructiveness of egotism.

Such a group or movement would be most iconoclastic and could therefore hardly expect to be popular. The more eloquent its insistence that we (whoever 'we' are) are not the defining centre of the world, the more effective its passionate and practical unmasking of idolatry and self-deception, the more it would meet with resistance. It would soon find that its problem was not that of trying to be fair to both sides, but of preventing the clarity of its message from being obscured by becoming the servant of any set of particular interests.

But why speculate? We do not need to invent such a group or movement. It already exists, and, by our confession of Christian faith, we acknowledge ourselves to belong to it.

Such acknowledgement, such confession, is not a claim to superior knowledge or special virtue. We are not gnostics or sectaries. On the contrary, our confession is, in the first place, confession of sin, acknowledgement of complicity in self-deception. It is, in the second place, acknowledgement that we cannot wake ourselves from sleep, acknowledgement that the 'unclouding' of the moral imagination is pure grace.

But far from such recognition of incapacity affording us the slightest excuse for 'carrying on regardless', our confession is, in the third place, celebration of grace already given, acknowledgement that forgiveness has the first and last word over sin, life the first and last word over death.

It is this clear-sighted joyfulness, this radiance, that is, I think, prophetic Christianity's most paradoxical feature. There is, in the light of Easter, a kind of singing even in Gethsemane.

Even in the heightened darkness of Hitler's Germany, there were those who discovered, as pure gift, and at great personal cost, that it was not necessary to 'carry on regardless'. Our prayer must surely be that we may make some similar discovery and, in so doing, release energies that would bear fruit, in ways that cannot be predicted, for the true healing of humanity, the redemption of the world.

At least, if we fail to do so, we have no reason to suppose that, in matters of world peace, of economic order, or the internal arrangements of British society, future generations will not judge our Christianity to have been counterfeit, will not judge us, in our most commonplace and undramatic wickedness, to have been complicit in our world's destruction.

Have I been too apocalyptic? Perhaps, and the church in Laodicea probably thought so too. But surely we still need to hear 'what the spirit says to the churches', and the message has not changed.

PREACHED BEFORE THE UNIVERSITY OF OXFORD,
17 NOVEMBER 1985

*Notes*

1. Dietrich Bonhoeffer, *Ethics* (London, 1964), p. 64.
2. John Harriott, 'The Darkness in All of Us,' *The Tablet* (5 October 1985), p. 1026.
3. *Ethics*, pp. 65–6.
4. *Ethics*, pp. 66–7.

# 11

# Wealth and poverty

Lamentations 2:13–16
1 Thessalonians 5:1–11

In March 1866, while convalescing from a severe attack of
carbuncles, he walked the seventeen miles to what he
described, in a letter to one of his daughters, as 'an old, ugly
medieval sort of town, not mended by large modern English
barracks at the one end and a dismal dry Railway Station at
the other end of the oldish thing. There is no trace of
poetry about it . . . Happily I was too tired, and it was too
late, to look out for the celebrated cathedral.'[1]

The 'medieval sort of town' was not, in fact, Cambridge,
but Canterbury, and the energetic invalid with vigorous
judgements was Karl Marx. I do not know with what mixture
of amusement, bewilderment and contempt he would have
received the news that, in this 'celebrated' place, a Christian
theologian would one day be invited to preach on the centenary of his death.

What interests me about the letter from which I have
quoted is not Marx's failure to find the cathedral, but the
tired man's sadness at the dreary and dismal character of a
city in which he sought, but did not find, some 'trace of
poetry'. However defective his aesthetics, or sense of geog-
raphy, it is as if he were asking, with the author of
Lamentations: 'Is this the city that was called the perfection
of beauty, the joy of all the earth?' (Lamentations 2:15). He
had, after all, walked seventeen miles to see it.

Beauty and ugliness, wealth and poverty, are antithetical.
But any merely abstract expression of the antitheses

between them misses the point. The point is, not that
beauty is to be preferred to ugliness, wealth to poverty, but
that the acknowledgement of such preference entails
accepting responsibility to work for the transformation of
ugliness into beauty, of poverty into wealth.

It is tempting to suppose that this project of transformation, or redemption, can be straightforwardly stated in
principle, however difficult it may be, in particular
instances, effectively to execute. We know what we have to
do: heal the ugliness and create beauty; abolish poverty and
create wealth.

But, especially in this season of Lent, we can hardly fail to
be reminded of how intensely paradoxical are both the project and the circumstances of its execution. In this season of
Lent, we prepare for our principal celebration of what was
done in him who 'had no form or majesty that we should
look at him, nothing in his appearance that we should
desire him' (Isaiah 53:2). And yet it is this poverty, this ugliness, that we celebrate as the richest and most enriching of
God's acts; as the place, above all places, of the appearance
of God's particular beauty.

In the light of such confession, what are we to make of
our customary canons of poverty and wealth, ugliness and
beauty, and our customary strategies for transforming the
one into the other?

In its shapes and sounds, its architecture, its endowments
and its music, this is a rich and beautiful place. The richness
and beauty of this place is a principal reason why thousands
of people come, year after year (from far further than seventeen miles away!) to this 'old . . . medieval sort of town'
with its 'Railway Station at the other end of the oldish
thing'.

But how does the wealth and beauty which draws us here
relate to that wealth and beauty which we discern and celebrate on Calvary?

The richness that attracts us here is, in the first instance,
a richness of artefacts. Not simply of physical objects: of
stone, and sound, and glass, but also of ideas embodied in

the stone and sound – for ideas are among the more important of our artefacts.

Artefacts are produced to be used, by human beings. To what use are these rich artefacts put? Even to ask the question is to be uncomfortably reminded that the wealth and privilege which produced this place was in some measure acquired, and is in some measure sustained, at the cost of the poverty and dispossession of those who neither made this place nor now enjoy it.

I am not creeping up towards some iconoclastic conclusion. Iconoclasm is only appropriate when artefacts have been transformed into idols; when the stone, and sound, and glass, which should form part of the language of human relations, have been alienated, torn from their human context, and made objects of veneration 'in their own right'.

The only appropriate use of artefacts is as symbols of human hope and the flourishing of the world. There is no 'glory' in these rich artefacts except they reflect the glory of God. '*Gloria Dei vivens homo.*' The glory of God is man come alive. It is this glory, this coming alive, which, in the light of Easter faith, we celebrate in the poverty and destitution of Calvary.

It may or may not surprise you to know that all I have been doing, in the last few minutes, is to reflect, in a Christian register, the 'dialectic' of wealth and poverty which Marx explored in several places in his writings.

He says of the individual whom we (correctly) describe as the 'rich' man that he is, humanly speaking, as poor as the poor man. The difference between them is that the poor man's poverty is manifest, whereas the rich man's human poverty is disguised by the appearance of wealth: the wealth of artefacts abstracted, as commodities, from their human use.

Marx looked forward (and it seems not to matter much, at this point, whether we call the vision 'utopian' or 'eschatological') to a state of affairs in which 'wealth' would mean, not mere possession of artefacts, but wealth of relationship, freedom and healed identity; a state of affairs in which 'poverty' would refer, not to material destitution, but (in a

fine phrase) to 'the passive bond which makes man experience his greatest wealth – the *other* man – as need'.[2]

It is the *dissociation* of 'matter' and 'spirit', artefact and
relationship, which is near the heart of the difficulty we
experience in appropriately relating the wealth and beauty
of a place such as this to the wealth and beauty initiated and
enacted on Calvary. We are, this morning, surrounded by
beautiful things. But whether this is a place of beauty, a fore-
taste or sacrament of 'the city . . . called the perfection of
beauty', or a place of sin and ugliness, depends upon the
use to which, in practice, these things are put. There is, perhaps, a 'trace of poetry' in this place, this morning. But
judgement on these matters is best left, not to us, but to others and to God.

In drawing on some ideas of Marx as a means of commem-
orating the centenary of his death, it is not my intention to
do anything as ridiculous as to propose him as a candidate
for canonisation, or even for the posthumous award of an
honorary doctorate of divinity.

I would merely suggest that the stimulus to recover what,
throughout much of Christian history, were commonplaces
of the need to integrate action and thought, matter and
spirit, artefact and relationship, faith and politics, flesh and
Word, may come from surprising people and unexpected
places.

The suggestion is, I admit, a subversive one. It is subversive of our attempts to transform the Church from sacrament into citadel; to transform the Spirit of God from
redemptive breath into possessed commodity; to transform
the Word of God from prophetic healing deed into some
warrant for our enduring inhumanity.

If we believe that, in this rich and beautiful place, God's
presence is to be discerned, his Word heard, this is not
because we suppose him to be absent elsewhere, or to be
silent in the surrounding city. It is because we believe that
this is where we may learn the language of that Word which
is to be heard and touched, in its transforming beauty, outside all those convenient barriers – of institution, form and

structure – in which, in our fearfulness and self-interest, we seek to imprison the freedom of God: God whose glory is the coming alive, in beauty and human richness, of us and of all mankind.

PREACHED IN KING'S COLLEGE CHAPEL ON THE OCCASION OF THE CENTENARY OF THE DEATH OF KARL MARX, 6 MARCH 1983

*Notes*

1. David McMellan, *Karl Marx: His Life and Thought* (London, 1973), p. 338.
2. Karl Marx, *Early Writings* (London, 1975), p. 356.

# 12

# Images of the servant

Isaiah 42:1–7
Colossians 1:15–20
Mark 9:33–41

In Matthew's gospel, the saying about the 'cup of water' comes at the end of a discourse intended to steady the nerves of persecuted Christians. It should be no surprise if discipleship, obedient service, engenders social division, conflict and suffering: 'it is enough for . . . the disciple [to be] like the teacher' (10:25), and, in the outcome of that Calvary-formed likeness, to find his life (10:38–39). The lines of division between discipleship and enmity seem clear: even those who sustain the servant in his work, who give him 'a cup of cold water . . . in the name of a disciple', will share the servant's strange victory (10:42).

In the Marcan narrative, to which we listened just now, the emphasis is on the character of discipleship. It is service, *childlike* service (9:36), not dominance, influence or expertise, which constitutes 'greatness' in the new order of things (9:33–35). What would such 'greatness' look like? How would we know who is 'on the side' of his 'lordship'? Well, consider – as an instance of its likeness – those who 'give you a cup of water to drink because you bear the name of Christ' (9:41).

Matthew's account speaks to an existing situation of conflict, in which the lines of division between 'us' and 'them', the disciples and their enemies, the followers of Christ and those set in opposition to them by the 'sword' of God's Word, are only too painfully clear. They cut through closest ties of family relationship (Matthew 10:35–37). But even such sundering, such suffering, is to be endured without wavering. Even in such surgery there is healing.

Or, at least, the lines of division seem clear. But (the Marcan version reminds us) if we suppose that *we* know how to draw them, we shall get them wrong, because the criteria, the standards of performance and service, to which we appeal, are drawn from a stock of values not yet upended by the odd logic of the cross. Autocrats and bureaucrats and busybodies invariably suppose themselves to be 'at the service' of those whom they dominate and badger.

However sharp and painful the conflict between discipleship and enmity, service and domination, 'Church' and 'world', it is always (in Newman's image) 'a sort of night battle, where each fights for himself, and friend and foe stand together'.[1]

This elusiveness, this indiscernibility of the criteria in terms of which 'the people of God' can be identified, and can find their identity, comes across in John's account of Jesus' meeting with the woman of Samaria at Jacob's well. From that holy and practical place (a watering-place) her people had drawn their sustenance and their identity. Because of that well, they knew who they were: it had been given to them by their father Jacob, who 'with his sons and his flocks drank from it' (John 4:12).

Now, to that place, comes one who, at the point of giving up his spirit, surrendering his identity, will say: 'I am thirsty' (19:28). He comes to the well, and says to the woman: 'Give me a drink' (4:7). Which shocks her, reasonably, because he's on the wrong side: he's one of 'them', a Jew, not one of 'us'.

In fact, his casual, practical request is even more disturbing. He asks for a drink, at Jacob's well, and all he wants is water. He's not impressed (to put it mildly) by the fact that the water comes from *this* well, from *Jacob's* well. A whole pattern of division and identity, of source and significance, is being disturbed. A cup of water is disordering those configurations of history and location, meaning and destiny, without which social existence degenerates into

anarchy. And he himself is (as he says to her) the inex-
haustible source of this confusion.

But there must be some criteria of demarcation, some
lines of division. How else could we discern the path of discipleship, the track along which lies the faithful following of
God's Word and way?

It's not that he hasn't got an answer to this question,
but that his answer only serves to enhance the sense of disorientation. The lines of division, according to him, are
to be drawn, not between those who worship on this mountain (John 4:20) and those who worship on another; not
between Jew and Samaritan, Catholic and Protestant, theist
and atheist; but between those who do, and those who do
not, 'worship the Father in spirit and truth' (John 4:23).

And where does that get us? How are we to handle so elu-
sive a criterion? However creative such disorientation, we
can't just stay with the confusion thus created. We have to
recover some sense of discernible direction.

Two of the moves that we might make (both false moves)
have long histories. On the one hand, we can short-cut confusion by reconstructing, in his terms, the patterns he
destroys. There are long-standing Christian traditions of
such unconscious blasphemy. They take the form of identi-
fying the worshippers 'in spirit and truth' with the members
of *our* tribe, our tradition, our denomination, our class, or
nation or power-bloc. And so, from their hilltops,
Washington and Moscow confront each other, like Samaria
and Jerusalem, in aggressive and paranoid self-assurance.

Alternatively, we can acknowledge, very humbly, that the
lines of division are known only to God. We would not presume to discern them. Every point of view has something to
be said for it. All that matters is integrity. 'Objectification' is
suspect. We continue to *use* doctrines, institutions, patterns
of worship, because we find them 'meaningful'. But to suppose them to be *true*, to be expressions and embodiments of
truth, would smack of fanaticism and vulgarity.

It is really very difficult to see why anyone should sustain,
even with a cup of water, these apostles of shapeless benevolence. They will, it is true, escape crucifixion: why should

anyone bother to kill those who have nothing disturbing to say?

The impression is given, in much recent British theology, that the fundamental disorientation of Christian faith and discipleship today arises from our dissociation from our past: from the fact that the authority of Scripture, the authority of church tradition, the authority of doctrine, the authority of church leaders, have all been irrevocably called in question, with the result that we no longer know from what wells we might draw our sustenance and receive our identity.

I would not wish to underestimate the gravity of these problems, which are not only academically intractable but which undoubtedly also cause many individual Christians, seeking faithfully to image the service of Christ, acute personal pain.

Nevertheless, I believe that problems arising from our perceived dissociation from our past will only receive appropriate clarification in the measure that we attend, with at least comparable seriousness, to problems arising from Christian dissociation from the human present.

In a building such as this, the cups that we give to each other contain blood. Water, of course, but the living water that springs from the side of him whose blood was spilt, spent, poured out for our transformation. The customary costliness of these cups simply celebrates the costliness, the costingness, of the gift they contain.

But what is the relationship between *these* cups and cups of cold water; between these 'images' of Christ's service, and whatever else it is that we, and others, do elsewhere; between our sacramental transactions and the sustenance and comfort that is brought (or not brought) by individual kindness, by social service, by economic structures and by patterns of aid and development between rich and poor, Europe and the Third World? And what is the relationship between the blood in these cups and the blood that is spilt

– not symbolically, but in simple, crucifying fact – outside
these walls?

According to one widespread and influential account of the
relationships between sacraments and secularity, between
specifically Christian images and artefacts, words and symbols, and all the other things that we do, say, make and
imagine, the Church's function in human history is to serve
as a place of refreshment, to be 'dropped into' from time
to time; a place in which to renew our strength, to be
'refuelled'. On this account, the Church's worship, the
ministry of word and sacrament, functions as a kind of
'transport café'.

One difficulty with this view is that, whatever may once
have been the case, and may still be the case for some
people, for an increasing number of Christians the model
simply doesn't work. They do not find, in the experience of
Christian worship, that enhanced clarity, that illumination
of direction and identity, that renewal of strength and
courage, which they expect to find.

Instead, they discover the experience of worship to be as
ambiguous and as 'flat', as threatened by loss of meaning, as
'the world' outside. If these are the springs of living water,
they seem to have dried up. And so reports are issued on the
state of Christian worship which bear a striking resemblance
to Egon Ronay's reports on motorway restaurants.

But perhaps, fundamentally, it is not the signs that are at
fault so much as our misperception of the relationship
between these signs and other aspects of our life and activity.

The weakness of the model of the transport café is that it
supposes that it is only here, in these strange and occasional
places, that sustenance is to be sought and found. Implicitly,
the model appeals to a doctrine of grace which has forgotten that God speaks only one Word, in whom 'all things
came into being' (John 1:3), not two. God did not speak his
word of creation into a darkness, a trackless waste, which
silenced and obliterated it, and then, subsequently, speak
another word – of re-creation and redemption. However

much we may need to distinguish between aspects of God's single speaking, he utters but *one* Word, in the utterance of which he makes all things, 'making peace through the blood of his cross' (Colossians 1:20).

The weakness of the model of the transport café, the place of occasional sustenance, lies in its implicit appeal to a doctrine of grace which has forgotten that God breathes only *one* Spirit, not two. God did not 'inspire' the void into an existence which collapsed back into formless chaos, and then, subsequently, breathe *another* Spirit, a spirit of adoption. However much we may need to distinguish between aspects of God's single breathing, he 'gives breath to the people upon' the earth (Isaiah 42:5), and 'puts his Spirit upon' his servants to 'bring forth justice to the nations' (Isaiah 42:1), by one single act of inspiration

On the one hand, therefore, it is not true that only in specifically Christian acts and experiences, images and artefacts, words and symbols, and nowhere else, is God's Word to be heard and his inspiration felt. God's word is to be heard, his image discerned, wherever he is at work, in the way of his working, across the whole wilderness of the world. Moreover, for all its bleakness, 'wilderness' is misleading. What we call 'the world' is, in fact, the land in which God both plants and gives the increase, the earth that we are bidden to 'garden', in the sweat of our brow.

On the other hand, if Christ and the Spirit are not absent from what we sometimes call 'the world', neither is the mystery of grace simply present, without admixture, on that hilltop which we sometimes call 'the Church'. We often expect too much, as Christians, from images and artefacts, words and symbols, which have, after all, been constructed by human beings as unregenerate as ourselves. There is something ridiculous about the spectacle of a group of people sitting in a patch of thistles, announcing it to be an oasis.

We who call ourselves Christians have been brought, for some strange reason, to confess our faith in one single mystery of creation and redemption. We have been brought to recognise one man as 'the image of the invisible God' (Colossians 1:15), and to hope for that reconciliation of all things which 'the blood of his cross' (Colossians 1:20) enacts, initiates and exemplifies. Our task, therefore, is simply to get on with the mundane and costly service of discipleship – healing the sick and setting the prisoners free – without expecting any clearer or more reassuring indication of what these tasks entail than he received in Gethsemane.

If we believed this, we should at least be spared two ancient Christian illusions: the first, that particular programmes of creation and redemption, of making and changing the world, of technology and politics, can be deduced directly from the gospel; the second, that Christian discipleship has nothing to do with these things.

I am not suggesting that specifically Christian words and actions have no place. Specifically Christian words and actions, images and artefacts, constitute that language whereby, as Christians, we interpret the one history which is our common human experience and responsibility. Only by the use of that language, in worship and proclamation, can Christian memory and hope, which is our specific contribution to the common human task, be kept alive.

I have been sketching an account of the relationship between life and liturgy, sacraments and secularity, which was summarised by the Second Vatican Council in the statement that the Church is 'a kind of sacrament of intimate union with God and of unity for the whole human race'.[2] It is an account which sees specifically Christian language and activity functioning rather as 'signpost' than as 'transport café'.

It is, I think, an improvement, but it still won't quite do. And it won't quite do, because it encourages us to see the 'secular' simply as that which waits upon our interpretation in Christian words and gestures. It thus overlooks the possibility that the grace of God sets up 'sacraments', 'interprets' itself, in that very secularity, or mundane humanness, which operates 'outside' the boundaries of Christian symbolism. It thereby overlooks the further possibility that our Christian language and imagination need continually to be purified through attentiveness to other 'forms' of the one Word of God, other 'images' of the one Servant and Lord.

Let me try to illustrate the kind of thing that I have in

mind. Matthew's version of the saying about the 'cup of water' speaks of it being given to 'one of these little ones' (Matthew 10:42). Mark's version does not explicitly mention the childlikeness of the disciple, but it comes shortly after the account of Jesus 'taking a little child' and 'putting it among them' (Mark 9:36). What does it mean, to describe discipleship, the obedience of the servant, in terms of 'childlikeness'?

Many of you will know Bill Douglas's remarkable trilogy of autobiographical films, describing – with precision and without bitterness – his upbringing in a mining community in Midlothian. In the first of these films, entitled *My Childhood*, there occurs a sequence of extraordinary power and simplicity.

On a table by the window is a china cup, containing a handful of flowers. It is springtime, but there is a coldness in the room, the chill that comes not with winter but with loneliness, poverty and old age.

Jamie, aged eight, enters the room and, with an apparently wanton gesture of destructive disregard for the one bright feature of the room, throws the flowers on the table. He fetches a kettle and pours boiling water into the cup. He pours it to overflowing, and his profligacy in such poverty shocks us, as did Mary's shock Judas in the house at Bethany.

With another apparently careless gesture, he then empties the now warmed cup, spilling it upon the floor and, taking the empty cup in his hands, looks up and turns to cross the room.

Only now do we notice that, in a chair in the corner, near where a fire might be, sits the one person from whose few words and continual practical deeds Jamie has received, in his childhood, sustained affection: his grandmother. She sits, by the fireplace, her hands resting in her lap. The child takes the cup, places it in her hands, folding them round its warmth, and gently folds his hands round hers.

It is, I think, rare for human gestures of affection to have the purity, the directness, which the child achieves. (It is, as

I indicated, a directness which entailed an apparent disregard for other forms and values: for the flowers and the scarce hot water.) It is even more rare, if not impossible, for the structures of concern, of social, economic and political relations, to exhibit a similar human purity.

That gift of a cup, that child's gift, is no 'mere' symbol, no image of something other than itself. It is, if we believe in the singleness of God's word and grace, a sacramental enactment or instance of that grace, even if only those of us who have learned to use the language of Christian belief would thus construe or interpret it.

If we believe in the singleness of God's word and grace, must we not say that such is service 'in spirit and truth'; that in such service we have to do with the 'real presence' of him in whose poverty the 'fulness of God was pleased to dwell' (Colossians 1:19); that in such service we can discern the meaning of that language which it is our responsibility, as Christians, not simply to 'house' but to enact?

PREACHED BEFORE THE UNIVERSITY OF EDINBURGH,<br>
28 FEBRUARY 1982

*Notes*

1. John Henry Newman, *Fifteen Sermons Preached Before the University of Oxford* (London, 1892), p. 201.
2. Dogmatic Constitution on the Church, *Lumen Gentium*, art. 1.

# 13

# 'A sword will pierce . . .'

Luke 2:25–35

At the brightest points of night in the Christian liturgy, at the midnights of Christmas and Easter, there is an extraordinary concentration of sense and expectation, a controlled power, an eloquent stillness, which finds expression more readily in music than in words. In the old Latin chants it was heard, at Easter, in the intensity of the '*Haec dies*'; at Christmas, in the verses from Psalm 110 which were taken as the Introit and Communion antiphons.

For both verses, the chants attempted to speak of eternal begetting enacted in time. At the Communion: '*In splendoribus sanctorum, ex utero ante luciferum genui te.*' 'In the splendour of holiness, from the womb before the daystar I begot you.'

Eternal birth in darkness, celebrated in our night-time, 'before the daystar'. God's birth-time is always in darkness, '*ante luciferum*'. The darkness of God's birth-time is the darkness of the hidden splendour of his grace. Follow the thought through: God's birth, in our time, always occurs in that darkness which precedes the dawn, precedes the shining of the daystar, the 'lucifer', the light-bearer.

But this insistence seems in sharp contrast to our recognition, as Christians, that this birth-time is past, that we remember this birth-time, that the daystar has shone, that we live now not in darkness but in the daylight of God's grace, a light which shines from the 'pastness' of Bethlehem and Easter.

This tension between expectation and memory, between

darkness and daylight would, I think, be pure, unclarified paradox if we just played with the pictures and left our predicament, our circumstance, out of account. But the fact of the matter is that the darkness in each of us, the confusion of passion and motive and understanding, the obscurity of responsibility and relationship, is but an instance and an echo of that pervading darkness which is not lightened by the labels we attach to it: natural disaster or infant mortality, oppression or exploitation, deterrence or apartheid. We do, most certainly, work out our ways '*ante luciferum*'.

And yet, in that darkness, we do, as Christians, confess our ability to live, joyfully, in expectation; our ability to celebrate God's birth-time. And this ability does undoubtedly derive from our memory of light's dawning. Nevertheless, it is a strange kind of memory, a memory of hidden glory, a seeing of things invisible. The light that shines over the stable at Bethlehem streams from the darkness of an empty tomb. It is, therefore, still in darkness that we celebrate the birth-time of God's glory, a birth-time that occurs, until the end of time, 'before the daystar', '*ante luciferum*'.

When we meditate upon the Canticle of Simeon, upon the song of one who had, in T. S. Eliot's words, 'eighty years and no tomorrow',[1] we tend, I think, spontaneously to concentrate upon the imagery of light, a light which Simeon had seen and lived to hold, 'a light for revelation to the Gentiles, and for glory to your people' (2:32).

Eliot was not, however, being simply perverse when he focused, instead, upon the old man's age, and upon the prospect of 'the stations of the mountain of desolation' and 'the certain hour of maternal sorrow', which lay ahead; upon present and future mortality and suffering. 'Now at this birth season of decease, / Let the Infant, the still unspeaking and unspoken Word, / Grant Israel's consolation.'

Eliot was not being simply perverse because, in the gospel, the lightness of the Canticle is set alongside the darker tones of Simeon's prophecy to Mary. What, in particular, are we to make of that puzzling reference to 'the sword', the sword that will pierce the mother's soul, the soul of her who images both Israel and the Church? There is no member of either people whose soul is left untouched by a sword that pierces Mary, the daughter of Sion. In piercing her, it pierces each of us.

Light and the sword, glory and darkness, splendour and hiddenness. The tension, or paradox, is inescapable. In a phrase of Paul Claudel's: 'In order to know [God], we have to bring our own being into a relationship with him which precedes the dawn – *Ante luciferum.*'[2]

The general sense of the prophecy seems clear, but I am still puzzled by that sword. So I turned to the experts – and that (of course) was an imprudent thing to do! I discovered that that sword had puzzled Christian readers of the text ever since Origen and that, in their puzzlement, they had constructed a bewildering variety of interpretations, the great majority of which quite certainly had little or nothing to do with whatever it was that Luke originally intended to say.

In Christian piety, the most popular interpretation is probably that which would see, in Simeon's statement, a reference to the '*mater dolorosa*', the mother sorrowing at the foot of the cross. But this can hardly be what Luke intended, for there is no evidence that he or his community ever believed that Mary was present at Calvary.

Even more implausible are those interpretations of the text which would find in it a reference to Mary's violent death, to the eventual shaking of her confidence in her son, to the fall of Jerusalem or to Mary's rejection by God's chosen people.

It is worth noticing that the common theme, in all four lines of Simeon's prophecy to Mary, is that of a judgement which divides or discriminates. This child the old man holds, this dawning light he celebrates in the darkness of his encroaching mortality, is a sign or instrument of discrimination. 'This child is destined for the fall and rising of many in Israel' (2:34). Merely 'being an Israelite' (or a Christian), merely 'belonging' to a people, mere appurtenance to a

culture or tradition, is no guarantee of a share in the salvation which this child brings. Being 'a member of the family'
is not enough, however close the relationship. Even the inti-
macy of motherhood is no such guarantee. The sword, the
instrument of discrimination, 'pierces', and passes through,
even *her* heart.[3]

There is, in other words, a test, a transformation, a changing in the ground rules of relationship, through which not
only each of us but even *she* must pass. 'And a sword will
pierce your own soul *too*.' The remark is parenthetical, indicating Simeon's prophetic certainty that she will pass this
test.

The history of Christianity is (at one level) a history of our
infinite ingenuity in constructing devices for evading such
discrimination, devices for deflecting the sword of divine
judgement. We would prefer almost any other road to the
knowledge of God, drink almost any other cup, rather than
this one.

But all such devices are, in one way or another, attempts
to evade the logic of what it means to be a follower of the
Crucified, attempts to find a path into daylight which does
*not* lead through the darkness of Gethsemane and
Golgotha. But there are no such paths. 'If', said Karl
Rahner, 'we gaze upon the crucified Jesus, we should realize
that we are to be spared nothing.'[4] This I take to be simply
another way of indicating the sense of Claudel's observation: 'In order to know [God], we have to bring our own
being into a relationship with him which precedes the dawn
– *Ante luciferum.*'

I said earlier that Eliot's reading of the Canticle seemed
to me to be by no means simply perverse. It is, nevertheless,
a disturbed and disturbing reading in which the stillness,
the urgently expectant joy, which characterises the
Christmas liturgy, has been transmuted into accents that
seem much closer to despair.

'I am', says Eliot's Simeon, 'tired with my own life and the
lives of those after me, / I am dying in my own death and
the deaths of those after me. / Let thy servant depart, /
Having seen thy salvation.'

Let thy servant depart, I have seen enough. Seen quite
enough. How to hold on, in darkness, towards the dawn, if
all I hold, this child, this 'still unspeaking and unspoken
Word', is all there is to hold on to? It is not quite despair,
nor quite the clenched teeth of stoicism. It is, perhaps, an
old man's desperate prayer. It is, in some ways like, and yet
quite unlike, that same child's own final prayer on Calvary.
Simeon, like Job, is almost as it were rebuking God for utter-
ing an 'as yet *unspoken* Word', rebuking God for coming
close to us in a form whose face is godforsakenness.

If there is 'more' than this, if the accents are to be so
shifted as to render even existence '*ante luciferum*' shot
through with joy, tranquil with expectation, the one thing
that we may *not* do is to 'force the issue'. If the accents of
our song are to be those of Luke's Canticle, rather than
those of Eliot's rendering of it, then we can most certainly
not *make* it so.

God's birth-time is always in darkness, always '*ante luciferum*'. But that darkness is, nonetheless, hidden splendour.
If it is to radiate, in our times and places, *as* splendour, we
may be the last people to realise this. The saints never know
their own sanctity. But, if we are faithful to the discipleship
of expectation, if we succeed (unknown to ourselves) in
bringing our existence into a relationship with God which
precedes the dawn, then others may find in us surprising
joyfulness, a most unexpected splendour, a kind of dawning or daylight in the darkness of the world which is as
unmistakeable as it is subversive of every standard calculus
of clarity, flourishing, progress or prediction.

In order for the Church, the community of disciples, the
community of those who sing Simeon's song, to be, in the
world's darkness, the '*lumen gentium*', the world's light-
bearer, or '*lucifer*', the place of God's radiance, it is not necessary that we should see it to be so, but that others should
be warmed and illuminated by the joy which radiates from
our obedience, from our faithful existence '*ante luciferum*'.
In that way is witness borne, by those who are not themselves the light, to that life which is the light of all people,

the light which shines unconquerably in the darkness that it
has, in God's time, overcome.

CORPUS CHRISTI COLLEGE, CAMBRIDGE,<br>
CANDLEMAS 1985

## Notes

1. 'A Song for Simeon', from *Ariel Poems*.
2. See Hans Urs von Balthasar, *The Glory of the Lord, I: Seeing the Form*
   (Edinburgh, 1982), p. 401. The quotation, from Claudel's 'Sur la
   présence de Dieu', occurs in the course of an extended discussion of
   his work.
3. See the discussion in Raymond E. Brown, *The Birth of the Messiah*
   (London, 1977), pp. 443–66.
4. Karl Rahner, *Theological Investigations* 16 (London, 1979), p. 22.

# 14

## Authority and impotence

Nature, we are told, abhors a vacuum. As a vacuum is created, the pressures build up to occupy the space, inhabit the absence. When the forces that sustain a social or political system collapse, we speak of a 'power vacuum' being created. And pressures build up to occupy the space with new forces, new powers. The collapse of the system engenders anarchy; and the forces that occupy the space frequently exhibit a dangerous simplicity: they lack the delicate complexity of the system destroyed. Tyranny and dictatorship are often the children of anarchy.

Patterns of human relationship, social and political systems, are, however, characterised by the exercise, not only of power, but also of authority. And if the 'space' that opens up when such a system collapses is sometimes a 'power vacuum', it is sometimes the silence in which no voice speaks with authority. Perhaps, therefore, we should also speak of an 'authority vacuum'.

Take a very simple case, that of the relationship between parent and child. In certain circumstances the system functions smoothly. The child draws its security, its values, its information, from the parent. The child lives in untroubled acceptance of parental authority. The system functions smoothly; a certain tranquillity reigns.

But it does not reign uninterruptedly. The child, in unforeseen and unexpected ways, begins to assert its autonomy, to challenge parental authority. It stamps the foot, refuses to obey. If it is old enough, the challenge is consciously expressed: 'Why should I do this, simply because you tell me? Why should I suppose that you are right, simply because you are older than I am?'

The system has ceased to function smoothly. An 'authority vacuum' is being created. What are the forces that are likely to fill it? On the child's side, a clumsily exerted and fragile autonomy. And on the parent's side? On the parent's side, the danger is that the force that builds up to occupy the space created by the collapse of hitherto unquestioned authority is the force of parental power: 'You will do as you are told, whether you want to or not, and, if you do not do it at once, you will go to bed without supper.' The parent wins because it is larger and stronger, and knows how to cook: the authority vacuum is filled with the exercise of power.

Too often, in our reflection on problems of authority, we fail sufficiently to distinguish between authority and power. And yet the distinction is fundamental. The parent, in my little parable, was *not* exercising parental authority, but exercising parental power. Authority is rarely, if ever, claimed or asserted until it is on the way to being lost.

Authority has something to do with 'authorship', and hence with the sources of truth, growth, vitality and significance. At least where relationships between adult human persons are concerned, the concept of authority always refers to a moral relationship, freely bestowed and accepted, between free and rational agents. In contrast, the concept of power may refer to sheerly physical, material relationships. I may have the power to kick a stone, or beat a donkey, but it would be odd to speak of my having authority over them.

Moreover, to speak of authority is usually to speak of moral entitlement. From the mere fact that I have another person in my power, it does not necessarily follow that they are subject to my authority. If it did, there could never be rational, moral grounds for protest against tyranny. Similarly, we may speak of persons acting with authority in situations in which they are powerless to produce the results they intend: this is a state of affairs with which not only parents, but also academic, ecclesiastical and political 'authorities' are frequently familiar.

Having suggested, then, that it is a mistake to confuse 'authority' with 'power', and having also suggested that, in crises of authority, there is often a danger that the exercise of power will be invoked as a substitute for lost authority, I would now like to consider a couple of more complex instances of crises of authority, of the emergence of that silence in which voices of authority are no longer heard as authoritative.

In the first place, there is the state of affairs that obtains when some particular 'voice' of truth or value, some particular authority, loses its credibility. Those institutions, or those individuals, that were previously trusted as the privileged embodiments of reliable information and guidance, of authentic value and significance, appear as questionable as the rest of us. And so we speak of a 'crisis of biblical authority', or the 'crisis of adolescence', or of 'political crisis'. And if, in a variety of different contexts, the Emperor now appears to have no clothes, it is *we* who feel naked, exposed to cold and uncomfortable winds.

In the second place, underlying the crisis of particular authorities, a deeper and more fundamental 'authority vacuum' may appear. The problem now is not simply that this or that particular voice of authority has lost its credibility, but that we become conscious of a darker bewilderment, an absence of criteria on the basis of which values are to be chosen, goals selected, truth affirmed. The problem now is not simply that we do not know 'to whom we should turn', but that we do not know on what basis we are to decide to whom we should turn.

Our sense of historical and social security is never so threatened as when all values, all meanings, and consequently all goals and policies of action, have been relativised to the point that the ascription of value, the discernment of meaning, seems purely arbitrary – a matter of taste. Like Matthew Arnold's traveller in *Stanzas from the Grande Chartreuse*, we find ourselves 'Wandering between two worlds, one dead, the other powerless to be born'. Even 'wandering' is perhaps too positive a metaphor, because it suggests at least that we are in control of our movements, whereas one of the most disturbing features of a fundamental 'authority vacuum' is the sense that the situation is beyond our individual or even our group control. We are, in the darkness, conscious of being 'acted upon', but apparently incapable of responsible and effective action.

Theologians are sometimes asked: 'Why do you make it all so *complicated?*' But cartographers are not to be blamed for the complex irregularity of the earth's surface. The irreducible complexity of human existence, action, relationship, organisation, is not something that is invented or constructed by theoretical commentators – be they theologians, economists, sociologists or philosophers. If there is anything in our situation that is simply given, if there is one 'brute fact' that is simply there, prior to all our puzzlement and reflection, it is the simple fact that 'it is all too complicated'. And it is, in no small measure, this perceived complexity that threatens our security, undermines our confidence that we are, or can be, in control of our sense or of our destiny.

Thus it is that, in the authority vacuum, threatened by complexity, we seek for simplicity. And the quest for simplicity takes many forms.

Sometimes, it takes the form of seeking to control events by imposing a shape, an order, on them. This is the simplicity of the exercise of power. The desire for simplicity is not infrequently productive of intolerance and tyranny.

Sometimes, it takes the form of seeking to reconstruct the supposed simplicities of the past. But because the past was not, in fact, as simple as it appears to be to our troubled nostalgia, this form of the quest for simplicity is in some measure arbitrary, illusory, evasive of reality.

Sometimes, it takes the form of closing our minds and hearts to the painful complexity of public fact, and seeking simplicity in some 'interior' or 'spiritual' world. This is the quest for simplicity characteristic of some forms of religious revivalism. It abdicates responsibility for public fact, and reinforces our slavery by redescribing it as spiritual freedom.

Sometimes, the quest for simplicity takes the form of ascribing absolute authority to some single authoritative particular: to one book, to one institution, to one individual. From the standpoint of religious belief, thus to ascribe absolute authority to any authoritative particular is uniquely to ascribe to that particular the authority of God. It is to affirm that only in *this* book, *this* institution, *this* individual, is God's truth to be discerned. But, by implicitly denying that *all* truth, wherever it is discerned, is a reflection of the truth of God, the God whose truth we do thus affirm is an idol, a creature of our mind's construction.

The various forms of the quest for simplicity that I have mentioned do not usually exist in isolation one from another. In practice, we select and combine them, weaving them together to suit what we suppose to be our needs. Nevertheless, they all have one thing in common: they seek a way out of the darkness of complexity through the construction, in practice and in theory, of single simple solutions. And it is the very fact that they are *constructed* simplicities that exposes them as illusory, as incapable of delivering the goods. For truth, and value, and security, and freedom are, in the last resort, not constructed, but received; not inventions, but gifts.

The question that confronts us in the darkness and disorientation of the authority vacuum is not: how may light, and meaning, and direction, be constructed, but how may they be found?

This strategic distinction between construction and discovery may sound very abstract. But consider how it is with human relationships; say, with the relationship of husband and wife.

There are, in any such relationship, periods of crisis, of complex disorientation. If the crisis is to be resolved in truth, in integrity, it will not be resolved by either partner seeking to impose pattern and order on the relationship, by dominating the other. It will not be resolved by the simplicity of power.

But neither will it be resolved by seeking to reconstruct the imagined simplicity of the past: the recovery of a romanticised honeymoon.

Nor will it be solved by either party constructing, in their heads, an ideal image of the other, or of the relationship, which does not correspond to the complexity of the facts.

Crises in relationship expose the fragility of that world of which I, the individual, am the centre. Such crises cannot be healed by any of the devices that we employ in order to reinforce that self-centredness, for it is precisely the egotism that constitutes the fundamental threat to the relationship. Only in the measure that the threatened and threatening egotism is destroyed, only in the measure that the 'centre' of the relationship is mutually displaced, can a new and deeper security be found that is never 'possessed', but has always, and always in darkness, to be newly received as gift. And this perpetual dispossession of the self is always dangerous, because it is not simply egotism that is at risk, but the 'ego', the identity, of the persons. And that risk is not illusory. It may be true that 'all we need is love' but, as a matter of sober fact, human relationships are exceedingly dangerous.

Although I have not so far introduced any explicitly theological considerations, I have had, all the time, at the back of my mind, questions such as the following. In what sense was Jesus 'in control' of his destiny as he went up to Jerusalem, as he trod the way of the cross? What kind of personal 'security' may we suppose him to have enjoyed in Gethsemane and on Calvary? What kind of risks did he undergo in doing what he did in the manner that he did it? When we speak of the 'authority' of Jesus the Christ, to what are we referring?

The gospel accounts of the temptations of Jesus seem to suggest that, in the 'authority vacuum' created by the failure of his ministry, he was tempted to fill that vacuum by the exercise of power. That he refused to do so is central to the purport of the paradoxical affirmation that he proclaims and embodies the power and authority of God.

In being faithful to that refusal he risked failure. And he

failed. And we must not redescribe that failure as success unless we are prepared, in our own action and speech, behaviour and perception, drastically to rewrite the grammar of success and failure, of authority and of power.

In what sense was he 'in control' of his destiny? If we simply deny that he was, in any sense, 'in control'; if we understand him as having been merely the victim of the religious and political forces that acted upon him, that destroyed him, we deprive his action of that centre of freedom which is insistently affirmed in the narratives of the passion. If, on the other hand, we simply affirm that he *was* 'in control' of his destiny, we falsify the narrative by depriving him of his humanity: a humanity that, in response to the forces acting upon it, risked, and failed, and was broken.

Perhaps we should say that, subsequently, his destiny was perceived to have been under control. Not under *his* control, except in the sense that he surrendered all control: that was the character of his dangerous obedience. Nor was that surrender the passivity of the quietist, who simply lets events take their course. His surrender of control, his relinquishment of security, was a course of action freely entered upon. There is an obscure sense in which we have to say that he was the agent in what was being done.

In reflecting on the sense in which that which we rightly call his 'passion' was nevertheless his 'action', and the action of him in whom he placed his trust, his sense, his 'centre', we move to the heart of the mystery of Christ. In that mystery, enacted and undergone in cross and resurrection, there is at once the denial that truth, security and freedom may simply be constructed, and the affirmation that, within our human history, they may be and have been found.

I have suggested that it is illegitimate to seek to fill the authority vacuum by absolutising some one particular authority: one book, one proposition, one religious or political institution, one individual. And Christians have often been tempted thus to absolutise the authority of Christ. But the security thus acquired is illusory: not only does it evade the irreducibly dark complexity of human experience and human suffering but, in so doing, it has frequently been responsible for fresh forms of intolerance and tyranny.

To affirm that the power and authority of God are uniquely embodied, enacted and exhibited, in the person and fate of Jesus, necessitates continual reconstruction of models of power, of authority, and of God. There is, within human history, no security legitimately *possessed*. Dangerously, Christian faith expresses and enacts the confidence that, across the whole dark texture of cultural, political and personal complexity, and nowhere else, truth, security and freedom are ultimately to be found.

PREACHED AT GREAT ST MARY'S, THE UNIVERSITY CHURCH,
CAMBRIDGE, 22 APRIL 1979

# 15

## Bethlehem and Gethsemane

Micah 4:8–10; 5:1–4
Revelation 12:1–6

The book of Genesis places the world's midwinter at the beginning. It was then, from primal darkness, unformed chaos, that God drew light, and shape, and leaf, and colour. We may, I think, today be equally inclined to place that darkness at the end. When we now invoke, as political cliché, Richard III's 'winter of discontent', we are not thinking cheerfully of spring, but of some darkening and freezing of the social fabric which may contain intimations of ineluctable decline. And even the optimists among us now glimpse, on the horizon of expectation, a darkness, a return to chaos, absolutely beyond seasonal reversal. There is, for human civilisation, no prospect of spring beyond a nuclear winter.

And yet, as we approach the beginning of Advent, the Church's season of expectation, we are reminded, this year as every year, that the date of Christmas was fixed in order to 'baptise' the winter solstice; in order to affirm, at winter's darkest heart, that the light shining from Bethlehem stands unconquerable: 'it shines in the darkness, and the darkness did not overcome it' (John 1:5).

How are we to fit these things together, bring these conflicting images into single focus? The general issue here, of course, is that of the relationship between our mundane human experience, in all its bewildering and threatening perplexity, on the one hand and, on the other, our attempts to make the biblical narratives our own story; our attempts so to appropriate those narratives as to make them our personal autobiography and the true story of the human race.

The great temptation is to suppose (and the supposition may take many different forms) that, in the light of these narratives, the darkness might be banished and perplexity scattered. If this is what we expect, then, when we find ourselves forced to admit, as a matter of elementary honesty, that – across the whole sweep of human experience, from personal mortality to famine and the prospect of global war – the darkness is unlifted and the cold unthawed, we let slip the biblical narratives, perhaps wistfully, as the fairy tales of infancy that give cold comfort to our maturity.

But surely this whole framework of expectation is itself exceedingly immature? There is, in our culture, a deep-laid and most unbiblical assumption that God's Word is spoken for comfort rather than for truth. If we could exorcise this assumption, we might *begin* to be able to bring our human and Christian, 'secular' and biblical, imagination into single focus. The results might be most disturbing. Death – our own death and that of all humankind – issues a veto against all attempts to stifle perplexity or scatter darkness. 'If', said Karl Rahner, 'we gaze upon the crucified Jesus, we should realize that we are to be spared nothing.'[1] But why on earth should we, disciples dozing in the garden of Gethsemane, expect it to be otherwise?

Many of you will have seen that remarkable film *Threads*, which was shown in September on BBC2. The 'surface narrative' of the film, you remember, was the destruction of Sheffield in the outbreak of nuclear war. The story began a month before the attack and, though the total time span covered was a period of fourteen years, the greater part of the film depicted, in harrowing detail, the time of the attack itself and the weeks immediately following.

Almost none of the reviews that I saw of the film seemed to notice the significance of its narrative framework. This framework was really quite simple. It had three elements. The story began, a month before the bomb dropped, with a girl conceiving out of wedlock. At the dramatic centre of the film, that girl gave birth and, at the end, the daughter to whom that girl gave birth herself brought forth a stillborn child.

The name of the girl, by the way, was Ruth. Now Ruth, you remember, married a man from Bethlehem, becoming an ancestress of the house of David. Nor was there always food or flourishing in Bethlehem, the 'house of bread', for the book of Ruth begins: 'In the days when the judges ruled there was a famine in the land, and a certain man of Bethelehem . . . went to live in the country of Moab' (Ruth 1:1).

Let's move through the waste land to the centre of the film, the point at which Ruth, 'a woman in labour' (Micah 4:9), is about to give birth. Knowing that the time has come for her to be delivered (cf. Luke 2:6), she seeks shelter in the desolate city. There are, of course, no inns. There is a barn, but the entrance to it is blocked by a large and savage dog, which stands, with sweeping tail, before the woman who is about to bear a child, clearly intent upon devouring the child when she brings it forth (cf. Revelation 12:4).

Ruth gets past the dog into the barn and, in this already familiar outhouse, she brings forth her child. There is, in her childbearing, no peaceable joy or romantic tranquillity. Many of our carols could not be sung in this night. The prophet Micah's song would be more suitable: 'Now why do you cry aloud? Is there no king in you? Has your counsellor perished, that pangs have seized you? . . . Writhe and groan, O daughter Zion' (Micah 4:9–10). After the birth, mother and child are seen surrounded by figures, formally grouped, showing no interest, happiness or adoration.

What 'king' is it whose presence is here denied? What 'counsellor' in this place devoid of peace (cf. Isaiah 9:6)? Throughout this entire episode, no words have been spoken. But, at the birth of the child, a date appears on the screen: the twenty-fifth of December.

Especially when we remember that the baby now born in such pain and desolation will herself, at the end of the film, give birth to a stillborn child, foreclosing all futures, we may be inclined to see the use of biblical imagery in *Threads* as resolute rejection of any attempts to alleviate despair, to

lighten the darkness of the prospect depicted. The message
seems to be: seek in these ancient stories some grounds for
setting question marks against the inexorability and ulti-
macy of our self-destruction, and you are evading the truth
of that black story in whose construction you are, by your
very evasiveness, complicit.

More sharply, the message might be: all *celebration* of
Bethlehem, all songs of starlight in a world bounded by the
absolute darkness of our actual expectations, would be, not
merely childish fantasy, but blasphemy.

The film can be read that way, and I think that, at one
level, we are invited so to read it. But there are also considerations which suggest the possibility of a rather different
reading.

In the first place, all romanticisation of the infancy narratives in the gospels – all attempts to insulate our telling of
*that* birth from the tragic dimension which imposes severe
restraints on how we may truthfully tell all other stories of
how individuals and nations, projects and civilisations, are
brought to birth – completely overlooks the fact that the
stories of Jesus' birth were first told as the *re*telling of the
stories of the birth pangs of Bethlehem, the travail in agony
of the daughter of Zion.

The birth of Jesus is not some romantic interlude in the
world's wasteland. It is told as the retelling of Israel's story,
which we are invited, in him, to make our own. And Israel's
story is a story of desolation and tragedy portrayed as pregnant with a promise whose achievement yet remains invisible and, *as* invisible, resistant to direct depiction. The
starlight, the glory, that shines at Bethlehem shines from
the emptiness of a tomb.

These considerations are at least hinted at in the film.
The date that appears on the screen at the nativity of Ruth's
child is not simply, as I suggested earlier, the twenty-fifth of
December. It is '*Sunday*, the twenty-fifth of December'. How
are we to handle the possibility that this opens up: the possibility that this birth in devastation is 'Easter-touched'?

Suppose we were to agree that, if we cannot make mention of Easter here, at the heart of the world's darkness,

then there is nowhere that we can make honest mention of it. Even agreeing this, we might still be tempted to suppose that the possibility of making mention of Easter 'takes the pressure off' the tragic. But Easter faith does not dissolve tragedy into comedy. The promise of light does not dispel the darkness. I am not saying that there is no difference between hope and despair. I am only suggesting that, contrary to the way in which we sometimes consider these things, there is no particular fact about our future which we know and Jesus did not. To live by Easter faith, with Easter expectation, is to be enabled to do, in the darkness, what Jesus did in Gethsemane: namely, to sustain, in that darkness, unswerving trust in God's invisible light.

All attempts to evade the tragic, in fantasy or speculation, are forms of self-indulgence. But there is another, perhaps more insidious kind of self-indulgence: a self-indulgence of despair. Chaos and unmeaning have their own seductive power. We are not, I think, immune, as Christians, from the temptation to indulge in a kind of experiment in masochism: the temptation to see how long we can gaze, unflinchingly, into the heart of darkness, without going mad. And so we watch the film, absorb the horror, and repeat – like a kind of mantra – 'Sunday, the twenty-fifth of December'.

Whatever such an exercise would be, it would certainly not be an exercise of hope or Christian discipleship. Nor do I see any reason to suppose that those who made the film did so simply to test our capacity for entertaining the unimaginable. Surely the intended purpose of the film was to provoke a response which would help to bring about a state of affairs in which the events depicted were less likely to occur? The function of prophecy, we might say, is prevention rather than prediction. And the appropriate response to prophetic utterance is 'repentance', 'conversion', change of life: the transformation of projects and policies, imagination and behaviour. This is as true, I suggest, of a film such as *Threads* as it is of the prophecy of Micah. But it is also true of the infancy narratives. If we forget this, we forget that they address us as 'gospel', as God's Word, as that 'two-edged sword' which 'is able to judge the thoughts and intentions of the heart' (Hebrews 4:12).

Bethlehem, the city of Ruth, and Micah, and Jesus, is not far from Gethsemane. In that child's birth at Bethlehem are 'represented' the wastelands of human tragedy, of human history as 'stillborn'. And, *in* that birth, these wastelands are depicted as pregnant with promise. Christian hope is an eminently practical matter: it is, we might say, a matter of transforming tragedy into pregnancy. Surrounded as we are, and as he was, by darkness, we cannot predict the outcome or depict its features. But we can, perhaps, learn to think, and act, and suffer, in trust conformable with the grace of him who alone can make the barren woman fruitful; of him who alone can make our Calvary the birthplace of his peace.

CHURCHILL COLLEGE, CAMBRIDGE,
18 NOVEMBER 1984

*Note*

1. Karl Rahner, *Theological Investigations* 16 (London, 1979), p. 22.

# LIVING AND DYING

# 16

## Ordering joy

Ecclesiasticus 11:7–28
Philippians 3:12—4:4

One curious thing about our use of Scripture in public worship is that we open other people's letters and read them as if they were addressed to us. (If there is anybody here this evening called 'Evodia' or 'Syntyche', I partially withdraw that remark.) To cope with this state of affairs, the biblically well-educated preacher then puts himself through hoops labelled 'exegesis', 'interpretation', 'application', and so on. His hearers are thus, he hopes, enabled to hear, today, spoken to them, that which was written, yesterday, for somebody else. I propose, somewhat barbarically, to short-cut this process, and simply to assume that we are, in some sense, entitled – as Christians – to attend to, and to seek to respond to, the texts that were read this evening as written for us, as addressed to us.

If we do this, then we find ourselves instructed, or directed, or requested, by Paul, to 'Rejoice in the Lord always' (4:4).

Now that is a very strange instruction. Ordering people to 'rejoice' is just about as helpful as telling them to 'stop worrying about it'. I am reminded of an exasperated choirmaster, snapping at his recalcitrant and lethargic charges: 'Rejoice, damn you!'

Joy cannot be summoned on request. Joy either is, at some particular time and place, our condition – or it is not. To be told to 'rejoice' is to receive an instruction which is either impossible to fulfil, or else is unnecessary.

But perhaps, since the instruction in question is a biblical one, we might take the request, to us, to 'Rejoice in the Lord', as in some sense a divine ratification or endorsement of such joy as is in us.

This seems to be the way in which Bishop Lancelot Andrewes took it when he said, in a sermon:

> To 'rejoice', no hard request nor heavy yoke, let it not be grievous to us. We love to do it, we seek all means to do it in all cases else; then to essay to do it here . . . And even as, when God calleth us to mourning by black days of famine or war, or the like, then to fall to feasting or revelling is that that highly displeaseth God, so when God by good days calleth us to joy, then to droop and not to accommodate ourselves to seasons of His sending, is that which pleaseth Him never a whit.[1]

So, on the assumption that this is a 'good day', a day whose goodness spontaneously generates joy, we have – in the scriptural instruction – ratification for our rejoicing.

But the joy that is of God, the joy that is the felt form of Christian hope, has a cluster of counterfeits – the range of noisy hilarities by means of which we wear the masks of joy to drown the silence of despair. And so, in the same sermon, Bishop Andrewes spoke of the need to '*order*' our joy – and he illustrated the counterfeits by recalling some of the more colourful biblical instances of a joy that is not of God:

'I come to the last', he says,

> how to order our joy, that it may please Him for whom it is undertaken. It is not every joy that He liketh. Merry they were, and joyful they thought, that kept their 'King's day', by taking in bowl after bowl, till they were 'sick' again. So they that Malachi speaks of, there came nothing of their feasts but 'dung' – bear with it, it is the Holy Ghost's own term – that is, all in the belly and belly-cheer . . . 'But with none of them was God pleased'; and as good no joy as not to the purpose, as not to please Him.[2]

If Lancelot Andrewes is right – if 'as good no joy as not to the purpose' – are there not some awkward questions to be considered concerning our criteria of assessment? How are we to know that our joy is 'to the purpose'? How are we to decide *when* 'God by good days calleth us to joy'? What is to count, and on what grounds, as a 'good day'?

These questions may sound rather abstract, but it is not difficult to give them concrete form. The sermon from which I have been quoting was preached by Bishop Andrewes at Whitehall, in the presence of King James I, on the fifth of November 1606. It was the first of ten sermons concerning the 'Gunpowder Treason' that he preached in the King's presence, on this day, between 1606 and 1618.

Now, knowing that, it is not difficult to see why James I, his court and his preacher, should have regarded this as one of the 'good days', one of the days on which 'God calleth us to joy'. The bomb hadn't gone off; the lives of King, Lords and Commons had been spared.

And yet, reading these sermons at a safe distance from the England of 1605, I find myself faced with those awkward questions that I mentioned just now, concerning the 'ordering' of joy.

Listen to the good bishop's assessment of the unsuccessful conspirators. 'We were delivered,' he says,

> and from a danger, that is clear. How great? for *that* makes the odds. Boldly I dare say, from a greater than David's. [David's] danger, he confesseth, was from man . . . This of ours was not; merely man's I deny it, it was the devil himself. The instruments . . . but a swarm of 'locusts' out of the infernal pit.[3]

The conspirators were not only sub-human; they were sub-animal. 'This', he says,

> is more than brutish; what tiger, though never so enraged, would have made the like havoc? Then, if the like, neither in the nature of men nor beasts to be found, (it is so unnatural) we must not look to pattern it upon earth, we must to hell; thence it was certainly, even from the devil . . . *Put to* all the cruelty in Jeremiah's

Lamentations, the not honouring the faces of nobles, priests, judges; the makers of so many widows and orphans . . . cruelty, more cruel to them it spared and left behind, than to those it took away. It irketh me to stand repeating these; that *ever* age or land, but that *our* age and *this* land should foster or breed such monsters![4]

The bomb had not gone off. Lives had been spared. Joy seems, indeed, to have been in order. And yet, if we heard that same sermon, the morning after some bomb had been discovered in time and had not gone off, preached today in a Catholic or Protestant church in Belfast – would we not be disturbed, would the integrity of our rejoicing not be threatened by the manner of its expression? Perhaps one of the reasons why, in so many situations, we find it difficult straightforwardly to rejoice; why celebration carries whispered suspicions of guilt or self-indulgence; why 'ordered' joy, rejoicing with integrity, sometimes seems unattainable, is because we have lost an innocence, a dubious innocence – we find ourselves increasingly unable confidently to identify our cause, the cause of *our* group, tribe, class or nation – with the cause of God, and correspondingly unable complacently to identify the cause of those who are opposed to us, who struggle against us, with that of the devil.

'Controversy', said Cardinal Newman, 'at least in this age, does not lie between the hosts of heaven, Michael and his angels on the one side, and the powers of evil on the other; but it is a sort of night battle, where each fights for himself, and friend and foe stand together.'[5]

This sense of the 'night battle', of the impossibility of separating the sheep from the goats, the cops from the robbers, arises partly from a deepening awareness – culturally, economically, politically – of our complicity in the world's evil. We are aware, as perhaps no generation in human history before ours could have been aware, of the unity of the world; of the seamless web of actions and consequences. For example, our prosperity depends, in no small measure, on the sale of arms that destroy people of whom we have never heard in the name of causes of which we are wholly ignorant. None of us – as individuals, as members of whatever ethnic, religious, economic or political group – has clean hands.

Perhaps one way of putting this would be to say that we are no longer able to say: 'this is a *good* day' – a day on which joy would be in order – *because* it is a bad day for somebody else!

Does it follow that there are no 'good days', that there is no 'joy to the purpose', such as 'to please Him'? I don't think so. But our awareness of complicity in the world's evil transforms our response to Paul's instruction into both prayer and the acceptance of responsibility.

It transforms it into prayer, because it becomes increasingly evident that the establishment of the conditions for rejoicing is beyond our capacity – it is the gift of God, the presence and transformative action of God's grace in history. Therefore, as the substance of our hope, it is the subject of our prayer.

And this same awareness transforms our response to Paul's instruction into the acceptance of responsibility, because it becomes increasingly evident that the construction of joy, and of the conditions for rejoicing is, under God's grace, the structure of Christian discipleship.

Joy, I suggested earlier, is the felt form of Christian hope. But Christian hope is God's gift, not our invention – whistling in the dark. Therefore, *as* God's gift, joy is to be waited on, asked for, expected.

And the joy that is the reception of God's gift of his life is, on that account, so much more deeply grounded than the fragile, divisive, destructive forms of its illusory counterfeits. As the reception of God's gift, joy is the translation into human experience of God's reconciling, transformative power. As the reception of God's gift, joy is established in human experience as that joy, for *all* people, which no one can take from us.

TRINITY HALL, CAMBRIDGE,
5 NOVEMBER 1978

*Notes*

1. Lancelot Andrewes, *Ninety-Six Sermons*, Vol. 4 (Oxford, 1841), p. 216.
2. Andrewes, p. 218.
3. Andrewes, pp. 208–9.
4. Andrewes, p. 210.
5. John Henry Newman, *Fifteen Sermons Preached Before the University of Oxford* (London, 1892), p. 201.

# 17

## 'I believe in the resurrection and the life everlasting'

Isaiah 65:17–25
1 Corinthians 2:1–14

A glance at your chapel card suggests that, alone amongst these invited to preach this term, I am to speak not about one fundamental aspect of Christian belief, but about two: 'I believe in the Resurrection *and* the Life Everlasting'.

If the Chaplain wished to convince me that he really had no intention of overworking me, he might say: 'Ah, but for a Christian these are but two aspects of one belief: to believe in the life everlasting *is* to believe in the resurrection – and vice versa.'

That is an attractive suggestion, and one to which I shall return. But, put like that, it overlooks the fact that, for many Christians who believe in a life beyond death, a life without end, an everlasting life, there are only the most tenuous of links between *this* belief and their belief in *resurrection* – whether of Jesus or of anybody else.

Thus, for example, when someone says that they believe that death is not the end, that there is, in human beings, a 'spark of the eternal'; that to be human is not simply to be material, historical, perishable, but also to be possessed of a life, a personality, a soul, that is indestructible, imperishable, immortal – such beliefs are often quite independent of the holder's views concerning the fact or meaning of 'resurrection'.

Many people, in many different times and places, have

undoubtedly been thus convinced that humankind is not only historical, material, perishable, but also in some sense eternal, spiritual, immortal. However, concerning such beliefs there are a number of things that need to be said.

In the first place, amongst the different grounds to which such beliefs have appealed, not the least influential has been the conviction that there must be an order of truth more stable, of justice more effective, transcending historical existence as we experience and undergo it.

In the second place, the mere fact that such beliefs are very widespread – that they turn up, in a variety of forms, in many different religious and philosophical contexts and traditions – is certainly no guarantee of their truth. Oppressed by injustice, victims of the arbitrariness of fate and heredity, human beings may cry for an order of effective justice. Threatened by the fragility of meaning, of peace, of love, they may cry for an order of imperishable meaning, of enduring peace, of abiding love. But, whatever the nobility of such a cry, it may go unanswered. The depth of our desire is no guarantee of that desire's fulfilment.

In the third place, beliefs in 'life after death', or in 'personal immortality', are not – or at least need not necessarily be – religious beliefs at all. They are, frequently, philosophical convictions of one sort or another. And if we seek to give them religious expression, we subtly alter their character and function.

Thus, for example, if I could 'prove' that I possessed an 'immortal soul', I would have something to 'hang on to' – some piece of security in the face of chaos. But if, as a religious believer, I acknowledge my immortality to be the gift of the Creator; if I acknowledge my indestructibility to be in his gift, not in my possession, then my security seems undermined: the suspicion lurks, like toothache, that the gift may be withdrawn.

In other words, belief in immortality often serves as one of a number of devices that we employ in order to evade, in practice if not in theory, the deadliness, the finality of death. We are afraid to die; we are afraid of that erosion, that crumbling into chaos, which is death the unknown as it threatens us. It would be comforting to be able to convince ourselves that we possessed some imperishable 'part'; that some constituent element of our personal existence was indestructible. It would be comforting – but would it be honest? It is at least worth noticing that Jesus appears to have enjoyed no such comforting assurance.

In certain circumstances, belief in personal immortality performs a function similar to that fulfilled by social and political utopianism. At least as an alternative to social cynicism and apathy, there is something invigorating and courageous in the utopian vision of an ideal future social order in pursuit of the realisation of which present struggle and self-sacrifice are heroically and selflessly deemed to be worthwhile.

The trouble with both these visions, however, is that, if you say that it is a 'future' life – life 'after death', or some utopia – that 'really' matters, you thereby deprive the present moment of significance. It is true that 'here we have no abiding city'. But does it follow that the city that we do have – the particular events and experiences and relationships and institutions that constitute our historical existence – does not matter? Notice that, if our history does not 'really' matter, then the history of Jesus does not 'really' matter either. That is the deadly logic of those forms of Christian belief which, puzzled or repelled by the fragile and paradoxical significance of one life once lived in time, in Galilee and Judea, avert their gaze from the scandal of the cross to fix it on some illusory future.

The scientist's tendency to dream, to fantasise, is disciplined by the obduracy of the materials with which he or she works. The religious believer in general, and the theologian in particular, too often seek to avoid being thus disciplined by the given, by the facts – allowing themselves instead the luxuriance of fantasy.

Sometimes such speculative fantasising takes pseudo-scientific form – as the contemporary passion for the paranormal, from Uri Geller or psychical research to *The Exorcist*, bears witness.

By all means let us investigate the paranormal. But if

anyone supposes that the results of such investigation could
have the slightest bearing – whether in the direction of
confirmation or of falsification – on the central claims of
Christian belief, then that person has fundamentally mis-
conceived the character and content of the Christian
Gospel.

One strand in what I have just been saying can be summarised very simply. It is speculative fantasy, not Christian
theology, to suppose that we have at our disposal any satisfactory description either of God or of the future.

The Christian, or the Jew, is in no better position than
anybody else to predict the future. I say 'or the Jew' to
remind us how easy it would be to misinterpret the passage
from Isaiah to which we listened just now. That passage
undoubtedly expressed a hope, but to suppose that it was a
prediction of the future is to suppose, for example, that the
prophet believed himself to be in possession of privileged
information concerning the style of life in some future city
which included a most improbable zoo!

Newman, in a memorable passage in his *Apologia*, spoke
of the 'curtain hung over our futurity'. In insisting that we
do not, as Christians, have at our disposal any satisfactory
description either of God or the future, I am insisting that,
for the Christian, that curtain is not removed or even ever
so slightly parted. Concerning 'what God has prepared for
those who love him', 'no eye has seen, nor ear heard, nor
the human heart conceived' (1 Corinthians 2:9).

That is all very well, but Paul – having quoted those
phrases from Isaiah – immediately goes on to say that these
things 'God has revealed to us through the Spirit' (2:10).
But before jumping to the conclusion that Paul supposes
that, in the gift of the Spirit, the 'curtain hung over our
futurity' is lifted, notice how the passage ends: 'But we have
the mind of Christ' (2:16).

This suggests that, if we would know what it might mean,
or not mean, to believe in 'resurrection', we have to turn
our attention to the death of Jesus.

In order to be able to say, as a Christian, 'I believe in the

Resurrection', I have first to be able to say: 'I believe that God has raised Jesus from the dead.'

Once again, there are a number of things which this does *not* mean.

In the first place, it does not mean that Jesus came back to life. This should not need saying, but apparently still does. Jesus' life ended on Good Friday afternoon, between two thieves. And that was the end. He never came back to life.

In the second place, to say that 'God has raised Jesus from the dead', is not simply to say that Jesus continues to live in our memory, in the memory of those who continue to be inspired by his life, instructed by his preaching.

He *does* still live in our memory, and that he does is integral to Christian faith and discipleship. Were his memory to fade, were he to cease to live in our memory, Christianity would be no more: it would have perished with the fading of that memory. But, when I confess my belief that 'God has raised Jesus from the dead', I am saying more than this. I am saying – to put it somewhat abstractly – that part of the ground of my belief that his memory cannot fade is the conviction that the statement 'Jesus has been raised' is an assertion about *him*, and not merely a statement about *us*.

But how are we to express this conviction? One quite common way is by saying: although life as we know it ended for him – as it does for all of us – with death, nevertheless he was raised by God to *another* life, a new life, untouched and untouchable by the corrosiveness of time and change.

This way of expressing belief in Jesus' resurrection has a long and honourable history, but it is not without its difficulties. Thus, for example, if we are to respect the 'curtain hung over our futurity', must we not say that we have not and cannot have the slightest idea as to what such language could possibly mean? And if we have no idea what we mean when we say certain things, might it not be wiser to stop saying them?

One apparent way out of the difficulty, which Christians have often sought to take, would go something like this. It is true that Jesus faced his death in darkness – in a darkness which threatened with destruction not simply his physical existence, but also the meaning and truth of the fundamental convictions by which he had unswervingly lived. But *we* know that God vindicated him – and therefore, in that knowledge, we can face our death, not in darkness, but in daylight.

I don't believe that, and for two reasons. Firstly, by turning the tragedy of Good Friday into comedy, into a story with a happy ending, such an account deprives the cross of ultimate significance and revelatory power. The resurrection is the *meaning* of the cross, not its aftermath – or the cross has no meaning.

Secondly, whatever it is that differentiates Christians from other people, it does not seem to be the case, in fact, that they are thus differentiated by being less darkly threatened by death, less destroyed by death, than other people. And we should not too rapidly assume that this is simply due to weakness of faith. We are bidden to 'have the mind of Christ', not to have a mind which he never had.

What then are we, who confess our faith in resurrection, saying or doing that others who do not share our confession do not say or do?

I suggest that this question can only be approached indirectly, by reflecting for a moment on what we mean by 'living' and 'dying'.

Is 'dying' simply a process *subsequent* to 'living'? Do we first 'live' and then 'die'? There is a trivial sense in which the answer can only be 'Yes': namely, that a person can only cease to be if he or she has previously come into being. But is that the end of the matter?

The process of dying starts, I suggest, much earlier than the moment of terminal death. Just as the physical constituents that go to make up this lump of matter, my body, are changing all the time – cells being replaced, hair and teeth dropping out – so also the relationships that constitute our world, our body, in a wider sense, are changing all the time. And here, too, the changes that occur often amount to irretrievable loss. Close friendships turn into Christmas-card contacts, and wither away. More seriously, by our failure to communicate, by our blindness and betrayal, we contribute daily to each other's dying. Dying is not just something that takes place during our last few weeks or hours. Just as our physical bodies, from the moment when they leave the womb, are set on a journey which leads, inexorably and ever more obviously, to senility and decay, so also it is true of the whole of our temporal existence that the process of living is also the process of dying. They are not two processes that succeed one another.

Indeed, without the willingness continually to die, human existence cannot 'come alive'. In our relationships with other people, with new ideas and the challenge of fresh situations, we have continually to risk the destruction of whatever 'safe little world' we have so far succeeded in carving out of chaos. The person who tries to 'hang on to' his life, to live 'privately', will die 'privately' – and this is hell.

The process of 'living', of 'coming alive', is also the process of 'dying', of corrosion.

It is not difficult to tell the story of our individual and corporate human history as a story of dying – of existence on a planet doomed to die. All it requires is realism and integrity. But what conditions would have to be fulfilled for us to be able *also* to tell the story of our existence, honestly and non-evasively, as a story of 'coming alive'? And how would we tell it?

Jesus faced his dying in darkness, but without ceasing to trust, to risk his future to, the power and love of him in obedience to whom he lived.

Jesus did not, and could not, predict the future. Neither can we.

To confess that 'Christ is risen', to confess that we have 'the mind of Christ', is to confess that we are enabled, by the God whose Spirit enabled and enlivened Jesus, similarly to confront all our dying.

Such a confession is not a claim to possession – of information, virtue or skill. Such a confession is not an entitlement to predict the future.

The language of such confession is the language of hope. And the grammar of the language of hope is the grammar of trust and prayerfulness. The joy which such confession embodies is not the spurious joy of utopian fantasy or illusory knowledge. It is – for us, as it was for him in Gethsemane and on Golgotha – a joy whose historical form is integrity in darkness. There is, indeed, even in the old Jerusalem, a song of the new Jerusalem to be sung – but there are true and false ways of singing it.

JESUS COLLEGE, CAMBRIDGE,
11 MARCH 1979

# 18

# Living and dying

Genesis 2:4–23
Hebrews 1:1–12

There are many ways in which the story of the world can be
told. The astronomer tells it in one way, the geologist in
another, the palaeontologist in another. And if we focus our
attention on that small slice of the story which is the story of
humankind, we can tell it as anthropologists, or as economists, or as historians of ideas. For the Christian, however,
there is yet another way in which the tale must be told, for
the story of the world is also the story of the world's creation
by God.

Christian belief searches for ways in which to express the
relationship of all facts and events and processes to the mystery of God. Creation is not something which God once did,
but which he has now ceased to do. The story of the world
is, from beginning to end, the story of the world's creation
by God.

But how are we to tell a story whose beginning is as obscure to us as the character of its ending? The story has
been told in many different ways at different periods in
human history, and the manner of its telling seems to owe
as much to the mood of the moment as to the amount of
information at the narrator's disposal.

A few decades ago, it was often told as a tale of progress –
from inorganic matter up the tree of evolution; from ignorance to knowledge; from the primitive to the enlightened;
from human subservience to nature and fellow humans to
control over nature and the liberty of fraternity.

Today, we are likely to be told the story in less confident accents. We have become more conscious, not only of the limitations of our achievements, but also of their fragility. The dark side of economic growth is ecological disaster; the dark side of technological growth is nuclear war; the dark side of political development is repression or anarchy. We seem always to be walking on the waters of chaos.

If we insist on taking seriously the dark side of the story; if we refuse to banish death, starvation, anarchy, unmeaning and violence to the fringes of some illusory optimism, how are we then to tell the story of the world as the story the world's creation by God? How are we to tell it as the story of the presence and activity of an infinite loving?

To put it another way: how are we to relate the two accounts of the story of the world – a tale of light *and* a tale of darkness, a tale of living *and* a tale of dying? This is no merely academic question because what we really need to know, if indeed the answer can be found, is: which of these versions is, in the last analysis, the more adequate account of the process of world history, of *our* history?

Where the history of an individual human being is concerned, we tend to think of death as the moment which terminates life. But this is a rather superficial view of things. The entire process of living is also a process of dying. Biologically, this is obvious, but it is equally true of that network of relationships that constitutes our history, our personal reality. Living and dying are not two processes which succeed one another. Death is not simply an irritating adjunct to the business of living.

But if this is true of the story of the individual, and of the race, and of the planet, then it seems intensely paradoxical to tell the story of the world as a story of its creation by God. What kind of creativity is it whose characteristic expression is destruction? What kind of loving could it be whose face is the face of death?

There is no way past the paradox – for the Christian or for anybody else. But the Christian is at least constrained to read the paradox in the light of the mystery of Christ. If we are to tell the story of God's creation in terms of this mystery of Christ, this means that we are to do so in terms of Christ's death and resurrection, of his dying and rising.

Good Friday came before Easter Sunday. Christ committed himself to the Father in the agony and darkness of death before the apostles discovered that that piece of history, the life of that man, had not simply slipped away into the past but continued to exist, radiant with new power and meaning.

It was only in the light of the resurrection that the story of Christ's living, and working, and suffering, and dying, could be told as the key moment in the story of God's creation of the world. But, *in* that light, every step along the road, every moment in the story, took on new meaning and significance. In the light of the resurrection, the failure of Christ's mission, his desertion by his friends, his suffering and death, could be told as forms of the presence of undying love in human history. The story of darkness could be told as the story of light.

If it is a mistake to regard death as simply an adjunct, terminating the process of living, it is equally a mistake to regard resurrection as a postscript to death. The process of living is also the process of dying; and the process of dying is also the process of resurrection. There is, indeed, an event of Easter, as there was an event of Good Friday. But, in the light of that event, the whole history of Jesus can be told as the story of his glorification, as the story of the 'homecoming of the Son of Man'.[1] In the light of Easter, the story of the world can be told as the story of an infinite loving without succumbing either to sentimentality or to illusory optimism. Not that the paradox is resolved by the Gospel. On the contrary, it is sharpened. But paradox is often the only way in which human language can pay respect to divine truth.

And we all of us act, and think, paradoxically. We dream dreams, we make plans, we look ahead – and we are right to do so. And yet – all the time, the machine is running down, friendships and moments of happiness are slipping, apparently irretrievably, into the past.

What is true of the individual is true of the race as a whole. Politicians, economists, technologists – make plans, ever prospecting (even in these doomwatch days) for a brighter and more prosperous future. And yet – all the time, natural resources are being used up, the machine is running down, the planet is growing cold.

This tension between two contrasting expectations is not necessarily irrational. It can also be our expression of the hope that no human achievement in time, however apparently fleeting or fragile, has been lost, and that even failure and disaster may be found to have meaning. This tension, in other words, perhaps expresses the only way in which we can coherently confess our faith in a resurrection which is not the postscript to death, but rather its transfiguration. It is the crucified one who, in the words of our second reading, 'is the reflection of God's glory . . . [who] sustains all things by his powerful word' (1:3). It is not for nothing that the risen Christ is said to bear the marks of his wounds.

KING'S COLLEGE, CAMBRIDGE,<br>10 FEBRUARY 1974

*Note*

1. This is the title of Karl Barth's exposition of the doctrine of the person of Christ in Chapter XV, 'Jesus, Christ, the Servant as Lord', of *Church Dogmatics* IV/2 (Edinburgh, 1958). The corresponding section in Chapter XIV, 'Jesus Christ, the Lord as Servant', is entitled: 'The way of the Son of God into the far country'.

# 19

## Faith in parenthesis

Private John Ball is a foot-soldier of no particular gallantry. He is the central, semi-autobiographical figure in what has been described as 'the greatest literary treatment of the First World War in English'.[1] But if we think of him only as 'infantryman'; if we classify him as 'soldier' rather than – more simply – as 'human being', we have already begun to miss the point of David Jones's great poem. 'This writing', says Jones in the Preface, 'is called "In Parenthesis" because . . . the war itself was a parenthesis – how glad we thought we were to step outside its brackets at the end of [19]18 – and also because our curious type of existence here is altogether in parenthesis.'[2]

At first sight, then, it might seem that the theme of this poem, this 'writing', is the warlike or conflictual character of this our curious existence. And yet, were we thus to describe it, we might still miss its message. Again, it is David Jones himself who gives us the clue: 'I did not', he says, 'intend this as a "War Book" – it happens to be concerned with war. I should prefer it to be about a good kind of peace' (p. xii).

The implication is that we are not yet in a place or a condition in which appropriate speech about 'a good kind of peace' is possible, except indirectly. Anyone can chatter about peace: church leaders, theologians and politicians do it all the time. But the hollow inefficacity of their discourse – the grammar of which wobbles between utopian prediction and moral exhortation – only serves to deepen our despair. I think that David Jones has helped me to see that, if appropriate speech about peace is possible at all, it is only possible indirectly, as counterpoint to the melody of war.

This is perhaps not so surprising as it may seem. As a Christian theologian, I should also want to say that appropriate speech about eternal life is only possible as counterpoint to the theme of mortality; that appropriate speech about Easter is only possible as counterpoint to the theme of Good Friday. It is not possible to speak truthfully of peace in abstraction from conflict, of eternity in abstraction from temporal finitude, of Easter in abstraction from Calvary.

The narrative outline of David Jones's seven-part poem is very simple. The platoon to which Private John Ball belongs assembles in England in early December 1915, crosses to France and moves up to the trenches in the front line – where they spend Christmas. In June, they are withdrawn from the front, moved south to the Somme where, in the attack on Mametz Wood at dawn on July 10, John Ball is wounded.

From the very start of the poem, our attention is focused on the ritual, liturgical character of the infantryman's existence. The words of command as they assemble to proceed to the place of embarkation are 'wholly swallowed up by the concerted movement of arms in which the spoken word effected what it signified' (p. 3). And, once assembled, 'they came outside the camp. The liturgy of a regiment departing has been sung. Empty wet parade ground' (p. 4). That Christmas Day, waiting and watching in the trenches, raw soldiers, not yet tried in battle, John Ball reflects: 'Here they sat, his friends, serving their harsh novitiate' (p. 70). And when, at the end of the poem, they make their summer assault on the German wood, in conditions of appalling sacrificial carnage, the sacramental motifs become more frequent, more urgent: 'But how intolerably bright the morning is where we who are alive and remain, walk lifted up, carried forward by an effective word' (p. 163).

But of what is this liturgy of ordered and most uncomfortable existence the ritual enactment? The first answer, I believe, is that war is the ritual enactment, the dramatic and symbolic concentration, of all that broader parenthesis, 'our curious type of existence here'.

To suppose that what occurs between those episodes of violent disorder that we call 'war' is a state or condition appropriately described as 'peaceful' is to have a most impoverished and hope-lacked notion of what would count as 'a good kind of peace'. Violence, oppression, heroism and destruction are permanent features of our curious type of existence. Sometimes these features are blurred, invisible, disguised by social structures and familiar custom. And then we say that nations, or individuals, are 'at peace'. But this 'peace' is hardly that for which we silently pray, that which we sometimes think we glimpse in friendship, brief tranquillity and the night-sky of Christ's nativity.

War and peace are related, not as successive episodes establishing the rhythms of our social history, but rather as permanent fact and fragile possibility, as circumstance and significance, matter and form. It is not only of soldiers in the trenches, at dawn on Christmas Day, that it could be said: 'Night-begotten fear yet left them frail, nor was the waking day much cheer to them' (p. 64).

The relationship at which I have been hinting – between war and peace, conflict and resolution – is not, I think, as outlandish as it may seem. A similar relationship obtains, in Christian experience, between time and eternity, mortality and resurrection. These, too, are related as fact and possibility, circumstance and significance, matter and form.

And, in order to focus and clarify, symbolise and confess, faith's reading of so-called 'secular' existence, the Christian community sets up signs: it dramatically organises and ritually constructs symbolic expressions of perceived significance and hoped-for possibility.

To put it very simply, I am suggesting that the relationship between sacraments and secularity, between liturgy and what we sometimes call 'life', is strikingly similar to the relationship between the rites of war and what we sometimes call 'peace'.

The really important question, however, is that which this suggestion immediately provokes: namely, are these two liturgies, these two ritual orderings of our curious existence, in worship of the same or different gods?

If you reply: 'the same, of course', then you stand in a tradition which links St Bernard's preaching of the second crusade at Vézelay to the blessing of nuclear submarines and the Ayatollah Khomeini. This is the reply of Constantinian Christianity, flourishing the wood of the cross as its battle standard. As I read the gospels, this is purest blasphemy.

Alternatively, we might say that these two liturgies, worshipping quite different gods, are to be contrasted as night and day, as the rites – respectively – of Satan and the 'father of lights'. On this account, the liturgy of war stands to Christian ritual as counterfeit to reality, as black Mass to the Lord's Supper. This reply, too, has often been heard in Christian history, from the monastic *fuga mundi* to the patient heroism of the Quakers.

As I read *In Parenthesis*, David Jones would have us resist either of these attractive simplicities.

At the end of the first section of the poem, as the soldiers disembark on the battlefields of France, there is a passage in which the liturgies are indeed contrasted, but with disturbing ambiguity: 'Toward evening on the same day they entrained in cattle trucks; and on the third day, which was a Sunday, sunny and cold, and French women in deep black were hurrying across flat land – they descended from their grimy . . . vehicles' (p. 9).

Or consider his use of an image which recurs insistently through the first half of the poem: that of the 'straight road' which leads across the plains of Flanders to the battle-front. Sometimes, this is quite evidently the messianic triumphal route of the returning exiles: 'Small hung-edges, and under-cuts, things just holding . . . found a level, – and small gulleys filled, and high projections made low' (p. 86). 'Follow on quietly No.7 – file in quietly – not such a pandemonium to advertise our advent' (p. 49). But sometimes the straightness of the road is the constriction of fate, the inexorability of disaster, rather than a figure of victory: 'Far thuddings faintly heard in the stranger-world: where no man goes,

where the straight road leads' (p. 30). 'The heavy battery...
as a malign chronometer, ticking off with each discharge an
exactly measured progress towards a certain and pre-
arranged hour of apocalypse' (p. 135).

There is a similar ambiguity in the use of images of flock
and shepherd. 'The officer commanding is calling his
Battalion by name – whose own the sheep are' (p. 2). That
is at the start of the poem but, well before the end, these
sheep, 'his little flock, his armed bishopric, going with
weary limbs' (p. 31) are lambs led to the slaughter, their
fleece impaled on thorn-bush of barbed wire. And when the
platoon commander dies (p. 166),

> He makes the conventional sign
>
> . . .
>
> He sinks on one knee
> and now on the other . . .
>
> Then stretch still where weeds pattern the chalk predella

– where it rises to the German wire. We are uncertain
whether he is priest or victim.

The simple solutions which Christians seek in their
attempts to relate the two rituals, the two liturgies – whether
by identity or contrast – too often achieve their simplicity by
abstracting from the circumstances in which the passion of
Christ, the paradigm of Christian action and perception,
was enacted. We have no title to a clarity of understanding,
or prediction of the outcome, which he lacked. The recur-
rence, in the poem, of images of Gethsemane is therefore
entirely appropriate. In the summer garden where the soldiers wait, before marching south, 'because they were very
heavy and their limbs comfortably disposed, sleep overtook
them one by one' (p. 136). And at nightfall, on the eve of
the battle,

> Some of them were already fallen to sleep, but the more
> solicitous disposed themselves in groups and stood about
> on that hill . . . and talk about impending dooms – it fair
> gets you in the guts.
>
> Let 'em kip on now and take their rest. (p. 146)

For Christian hope, or at least for an incarnational form of that hope, redemption, liberation, the achievement of 'a good kind of peace', occurs not outside time or in its simple cancellation, but in the very flesh of historical human action and decision. The grace of God is pure gift, and yet the reception of that gift is in strenuous engagement. We speak of the 'passion' of Christ, of that which he underwent. And yet that passion engenders hope because we believe the manner of its undergoing to have been nonetheless effective agency.

*In Parenthesis* explores this paradox and the dark ambiguities to which it gives rise. In a sermon preached in this church a hundred and forty years ago John Henry Newman used similar imagery for similar purpose. 'A soldier', he said,

> comes more nearly than a king to the pattern of Christ. He not only is strong, but he is weak. He does and he suffers. He succeeds through a risk. Half his time is on the field of battle, and half of it on the bed of pain. And he does this for the sake of others . . . we gain by his loss; we are at peace by his warfare. And yet there are great drawbacks here also . . . the soldier is but an instrument directed by another; he is the arm, he is not the head . . . His office is wanting in dignity, and accordingly we associate it with the notion of brute force . . . and violence, and sternness, and all those qualities which are brought out when mind, and intellect, and sanctity, and charity, are away.[3]

The ambiguities of human action, individually and institutionally, would be easier to bear if we clearly understood what was being made in our history and had some detailed vision of the outcome. But the vision of hope is bounded by what Newman called the curtain hung over our futurity.[4] For us, as for Jesus in Gethsemane, hope in the darkness is no stranger to fear.

As the soldiers march towards the front, just before Christmas, they stop to let a train pass: 'Trucks filled with very new clean deal planking . . . iron and wood and iron, made evidently to some precise requirement, shaped to some usage yet unknown to any of that halting company' (pp. 19–20). Six months later, on the night before the battle, John Ball heard 'the noise of carpenters, as though they builded some scaffold for a hanging – hammered hollowly' (p. 138). 'John Ball heard the noise of the carpenters where he squatted to clean his rifle. Which hammering brought him disquiet more than the foreboding gun-fire which gathered intensity with each half-hour. He wished they'd stop that hollow tap-tapping. He'd take a walk' (pp. 138–9).

A few years ago, a friend asked David Jones 'what the hammering was that Ball dreaded more than gun-fire. He replied, "They were making coffins . . ."' The friend said that he 'thought the hammering related to the image of the gallows-cross. [Jones] answered, "O yes, all of that. In the poem it is ambiguous. Ball didn't know what was being made."'[5]

We should not be surprised if our recognition – in the breaking of bread – of what was being made on Calvary, is fragile and fragmentary. The road to Emmaus and the *via dolorosa* both lead out from the old Jerusalem, the city we inhabit with fitful security, towards some frontier. But they are not *two* roads, going in different directions. To walk the straight road to Emmaus is to walk the *via dolorosa* in company and with lightened load. 'Their progress', says David Jones, 'was without event . . . they momentarily had view of . . . the road they walked on in the darkness of the night before. Most of them failed to recognize this landmark and were at a loss as to their position and precise direction . . . You live by faith alright in these parts' (p. 87).

PREACHED BEFORE THE UNIVERSITY OF OXFORD,
21 OCTOBER 1979

*Notes*

1. Thomas Dilworth, *The Liturgical Parenthesis of David Jones* (London, 1963), p. 3. At many places in this sermon, I am indebted to Dilworth's reading of the poem.
2. David Jones, *In Parenthesis* (London, 1937), p. xv.
3. John Henry Newman, *Sermons on Subjects of the Day* (London, 1869), pp. 57–8.
4. See Newman, *Apologia Pro Vita Sua* (London: Fontana, 1964), p. 278. The passage occurs early in the 'General Answer to Mr Kingsley'.
5. Dilworth, p. 34.

# 20

## Sewers and river systems

Genesis 2:4b–25
John 3:1–12

That second chapter of Genesis, that garden story, to which we listened just now, has been read in an amazing variety of ways. Sometimes, it has been taken as nostalgia, as the futile invention in memory of a never-never land, a non-existent dreamtime. On strictly historical grounds, however, it would be wiser to suppose that it expresses tough-minded hope, not soft-headed wistfulness. It was produced by people whose trust in the promises of God endured the comprehensive bleakness of their circumstance.

The *message* of this passage, its *announcement*, is: 'Nevertheless', 'notwithstanding these circumstances . . .' And if we suppose that its idiom, of 'Once upon a time', is unsuited to this purpose, then we have forgotten the way that fairy stories work.

'A river flows out of Eden to water the garden, and from there it divides and becomes four branches' (2:10). An immense amount of ingenuity has been expended in attempts to fit this description to the face of things – to sort out what Karl Barth called this 'hydrographically impossible and geographically indefinite river system'.[1]

We have, perhaps, the privilege (in 1990) of being quite unable to escape the force of the story's paradox: of these four rivers that take their rise in Eden, in God's garden of delight, 'the fourth', says Scripture, 'is the Euphrates' (2:14).

Part of the dangerous energy building up, at present, round the northern Gulf, is Saddam Hussein's attempt to blend together, in the imagination of a nation which we invented in 1921, every available trace of glory from Mesopotamia's past. There was a medal struck, a year or so ago, on which the profile of Saddam Hussein was superimposed on that of Nebuchadnezzar. The medal celebrated a music festival in Babylon: Babylon invented or rebuilt, at vast expense, during the height of the Iran–Iraq war. To focus patriotic celebration in this festival, no effort or expense was spared. The State Department in Washington (I am told) was asked to arrange, as star spot of the show, the finest flower of American culture. President Hussein was asked quite what or whom he had in mind. The answer (apparently) was: Madonna. Meanwhile, it is possible, in Baghdad today, to purchase Ishtar refrigerators.

'A river flows out of Eden to water the garden.' In part, it flows around the 'land of Havilah, where there is gold' (2:11). Or oil, perhaps. This river, this Euphrates, which the text presents as life-giving, copious, wellspring from the very heart of God, may soon again be bearing, sluggishly, its sad grey cargo of corpses; bringing not life and food and freshness, but the detritus of warfare, the flotsam of all our pride and fearfulness and greed.

But, to make the point again, it has *always* been so – from the beginning. This lyrical description of the river, this magic story of the garden-land of God, is told today, as it was told at its first telling, against the background of the desert: of the deadliness, the warfare, and the poverty of the world.

One way of putting this would be to say that telling the story of creation, naming the world as paradise, is always a matter of giving expression to our hope in God. And this, both practically and theoretically, it is intensely difficult to do, because it is a matter of correlating, without collapsing into contradiction, the paradox of life and death, of tragedy and celebration, desert and garden, dry bones and the movement of the Spirit. Nicodemus' question was extremely sensible: 'How can anyone be born after having grown old?' (3:4).

Karl Barth pointed out that whereas, in this second creation story, in Genesis chapter 2, water is the lifeline between the world and God, the image of God's Spirit, in the previous story, in chapter 1, it is the face of chaos: dark and formless, needing God's firm hand to hold it back and keep it in its place.

It is, I think, obvious that there is no question of being able simply to choose *one* of these accounts as true. If we shift, unstably, somewhere between despair and hope, between stoic acceptance and tranquil celebration, it is because we know that *both* accounts are true: that terror is as tangible as assurance, enmity as real as friendship, darkness as familiar as light. Even the oasis dweller, we might say, knows he is not quite safe, stirs in his sleep, as the night wind blows in from the desert. We know the truth in both accounts. What we find difficult is their appropriate correlation.

There are (to simplify) two ways of dealing with the paradox of dark and light, of wilderness and God's good garden. We can set the matter up either in terms of options that engage our hearts and minds and actions, or as episodes in a single story – a story with a happy ending. (Our preference for the latter strategy reinforces the suspicion that Christians are comedians, unable to bear the burden of the tragic.)

Thus, for example, think of the challenge as it sounds in the Book of Deuteronomy: 'Standing where you are, finding yourself in this particular set of circumstances, not of your devising – which way will you move: right or left? which is your choice: for life or death?'[2]

In contrast, we tend to say that now there may be darkness, but then there will be light; now we are nomads and wanderers, vulnerable to drought and storm and enemies, but then we shall live in plenty and at peace. First there was formlessness, and then construction; first weakness, but then strength; first there was death, but then came resurrection.

Fine, but how is this tale, as told, to fit the dark familiar facts? Or, as Nicodemus put it: 'How can anyone be born after having grown old?'

To try to sort things out a little, the place to which we have to turn, as Christians, is, of course, just outside Jerusalem. It is along the road to Emmaus, in trying to get some sense of Jesus' fate, in trying to discover something of how it went with him, that we get such purchase as we can on the story of the world as God's creation.

Jesus died. His story ended. Of course it did, he was a human being. The announcement that a human being has died does not invite the question (in Jesus' case, or anybody else's): 'Oh yes, and what did he do *next?*'

That is the first point, which anyone can make. But it's important. Jesus died. The second is this: we only begin to glimpse the strangeness of the Christian story, the curious grammar of its 'nevertheless', when we notice that, according to that story, the garden comes before the wilderness: life precedes and circumscribes mortality.

Dead men do not do deeds. Jesus died, was buried, silenced, still, and solitary. No light shines in the tomb; its darkness stifles all such silly questions as: 'and what did he do next?'

It is, therefore, dangerous to speak of Christ's 'experience' of death – because to do so may lull us into supposing him still to be alive. But we must take the risk – carefully, hesitantly – as the Fathers of the Church did when they invoked the paradoxical notion of the *visio mortis* – the 'vision of death'. What could the object of such vision be? No sign of life, no sunlit uplands – that's for sure! But, on the other hand, neither could that vision be of populous inferno, burning or ice-cold torture, because that would make of Christ's vision a contemplation of defeat.

Only one option left, an option proposed by Plato and Plotinus, and adopted by some of the Fathers. Death has *no* 'form', it is the shapeless putrefaction of 'chaos' (again!). The Greek word was *borboros* – mud, ordure; Origen spoke about the 'privy' of the world. There is no nightmare, no 'nothing' come again, no terror glimpsed by Nietzsche, that is unplumbed, untouched, in Jesus' dying.

And yet – not 'and *then*', but 'nevertheless!' – remember whom, as Christians, we claim this man to be. If this dead, unlovely stillness is the silence of God's eternal Word, it must surely (as it were) reverberate?

To say that *this* man died is to answer Nicodemus' question, because saying it announces that the endlessly creative wellspring, river of God's love, flows even here, contains and irrigates and transforms even this dry ground. Old men are born because God's youth is even older, went before. Gaze, if you have the courage, on the darkest, deadliest thing you dread: 'Nevertheless' – even this chaos is held, determined, rendered relative, made transient, by God's particular fertile care.

The power of this 'nevertheless', its resilience, is the power of the always previously outpoured Spirit. What it is *not,* however, is explanatory power. The Christian is as baffled and as heartbroken by the darkness of the world as anybody else.

There may be people who take the world to be a fundamentally friendly place, awash with reasonable grounds for optimism. I would not wish to disturb such people's slumbers (unless they appeared to be suffocating other people, on whose sufferings they sleep). But, as a Christian theologian, I am more interested in trying to help the hope and courage of those who know themselves, and all of us, to be – shall we say – in it up to our necks!

In Mesopotamia, in the months ahead, there may well be much weeping, much brokenheartedness, much devastation of structure and relationship. What, in such circumstances, we as Christians are enabled and required to announce and to enact, is that *nevertheless* it is still from *Eden,* from God's garden of delight, that the Euphrates, Spirit-water, flows – bringing old men to birth again.

MAGDALENE COLLEGE, CAMBRIDGE,
28 OCTOBER 1990

*Notes*

1. Karl Barth, *Church Dogmatics* III/1 (Edinburgh, 1958), p. 280.
2. See, for example, Deuteronomy 30:15–20.

# GOD'S WORK

# 21

## Mercy

Luke 6:36–38

Somebody who went to see *The Merchant of Venice* for the first time, and had not read the play before, would probably be deeply impressed by Portia's famous speech in Act IV. She acknowledges that, legally, Shylock has Antonio in a stranglehold; she acknowledges the justice of his claim, and movingly appeals to him to model his behaviour on that of the highest form of justice. Mercy, she says, is an 'attribute of God himself; / And earthly power doth then show likest God's, / When mercy seasons justice'.

The trouble is that, knowing the play as we do, the speech leaves a nasty taste in the mouth. We know what Portia is up to. For me, at any rate, the give-away comes later in the same scene, when the now triumphant Portia turns on the Jew and says: 'Down, therefore, and beg mercy of the duke.' The whole context and pattern of relationships which can thus force the Jew onto his knees, cringing before the Duke, begging for the exercise of an attribute which was earlier described as divine, frankly turns my stomach against the concept of justice, the concept of mercy and, in the last analysis, against the concept of God which seem to be involved.

What worries me is that the current English usage of the word 'mercy' still seems to reflect the same pattern. At least this is the case if popular dictionary definitions can be assumed to convey the usage of a word in the society in which they are written. One such dictionary defines mercy as: 'Abstention from the infliction of suffering on the part

of one who has the right or power to inflict it'. That
definition seems too close for comfort to Portia's concep-
tion of mercy.

'Down, therefore, and beg mercy of the duke.' Suppose
Shylock had done so; suppose that he had flung himself
before the duke; what would he have said? Perhaps something like: 'Duke, have mercy', or 'Lord, have mercy'.

That's interesting. '. . . earthly power doth then show likest God's, / When mercy seasons justice.' Is it not possible
that some Christians at prayer, praying '*Kyrie eleison*', 'Lord,
have mercy', employ an image of God, an image of our relationship to God, which would make the Father of our Lord
Jesus Christ bear an uncanny resemblance to the Duke of
Venice?

If this is so; if the best we can hope for, in our dealings
with God, is the reluctant magnanimity of a Renaissance
despot, what on earth are we going to make of our Lord's
command: 'Be merciful, just as your Father is merciful'
(Luke 6:36)? If the Church's style of life in the world is to be
modelled upon the attributes of God, it would seem that the
Church, or the individual Christian, could only be merciful
from a standpoint of unimpeachable moral superiority to
which few of us, I hope, would be willing to lay claim?
Something seems to have gone wrong.

Since Portia seems to have been a rather unfruitful source
from which to discover what the meaning of mercy might be
for a Christian, let's try another witness. Mr Gladstone, in a
footnote to his edition of Bishop Butler's *Sermons*, says that:
'Mercy is lenient and tender dealing. All compassion is
mercy: but all mercy is not compassion. Mercy looks more at
the case; compassion more at the person.'[1] Without bother-
ing in detail about the distinction he proposes between
mercy and compassion, the very fact that Gladstone sees the
two as being so closely related seems to be an improvement.
To have compassion; to be compassionate; tenderly and lov-
ingly to suffer with another. To be compassionate is not to
render some service which leaves the giver untouched. It is,
quite simply, to be *with* the person in their suffering; to suffer with them. Such a relationship implies neither moral

superiority nor the isolation of power. And while it is possible to trivialise the concept of compassion by sentimentalising it, at least it escapes that undertone of lofty inhumanity which disfigures Portia's picture of the merciful judge.

The reason why I have approached the concept of mercy by a detour through Shakespeare and, even more improbably, a British Prime Minister, is that I wanted to try to get out of the way at least one possible misunderstanding of what the Bible means when it speaks of the mercy of God, and of that quality of human behaviour which would at once refract and embody the divine mercy in human affairs.

One obvious New Testament text for us to consider, a text flagrantly misused by polemicists of various sorts throughout the nineteenth century, is our Lord's quotation from Hosea: 'I desire mercy, not sacrifice' (Matthew 9:13). I took a sort of Gallup Poll of some modern English translations of the Bible, and the result was rather interesting. All the translations of the New Testament at which I looked used the word 'mercy'. On the other hand, when I turned to the same passage in the Old Testament, to the prophecy of Hosea itself, *none* of them used the word 'mercy'. There, the same word was translated as 'love' or 'steadfast love'.[2]

We are now in an altogether different world from the court of Venice. It just wouldn't make sense to say: 'Down, therefore, and beg steadfast love of the duke.' In other words, if we are going to discover the meaning of God's mercy, as the Bible speaks of it; if we are going to discover how to be obedient to Christ's command to 'Be merciful, just as your Father is merciful', it may be necessary, paradoxically, to get the word 'mercy' out of our heads.

To confess God as merciful is to confess the unshakeable fidelity of the kindness of God, as it has shown itself in human freedom. To confess God as merciful is to confess, not merely – in the abstract – that in his steadfast love he wills to save, but, in the concrete, that he saves; that he has set people free. (This is the way that Psalm 136, for example, goes about it.) To know the mercy of God is to know that God, in his steadfast love, is 'compassioning'; that he suffers in silence in the suffering of human beings. To know the mercy of God is to have been in the garden of Gethsemane. It is to say of Christ, as the letter to the Hebrews does, that 'he had to become like his brothers and sisters in every respect, so that he might be a merciful and faithful high priest in the service of God' (Hebrews 2:17). (It is significant that the Jerusalem Bible translates that phrase as 'a compassionate and trustworthy high priest'.)

Now it becomes possible, I think, to see what is meant by the command 'Be merciful, just as your Father is merciful.' The Church is commanded by Christ to suffer with the world; to be there, at the centre of the world's Gethsemane, wherever people are to be set free. And if the word 'mercy' inhibits our discovery of the meaning of the mercy of God, so do phrases such as 'works of mercy'. Such phrases too often imply that immunity, that superior beneficence, which we discarded earlier. God's work of mercy is the cross of Christ. Christ did not *deign* to die; he was simply there, stretched on the cross, bleeding between two thieves.

The non-Christian world is tired of the words of Christians. The world is tired of sentiments of general benevolence uttered from a safe distance. 'Be merciful, just even as your Father is merciful.' Wherever people suffer, wherever they are oppressed and humiliated, there is the place of the Church. There, and nowhere else, can the mercy of God be proclaimed in necessary silence.

Let's go back to Shylock again and, in this passage, replace the word 'Jew' in your own minds by words like 'black' and 'poor' and 'homeless' and 'unemployed': 'Hath not a Jew eyes? hath not a Jew hands . . . fed with the same food, hurt with the same weapons, subject to the same diseases, healed by the same means, warmed and cooled by the same winter and summer, as a Christian is?'³

That is an appeal for mercy. To the extent that the Church evades such an appeal, it stands under the judgement of a merciful God.

SIDNEY SUSSEX COLLEGE, CAMBRIDGE,<br>
26 OCTOBER 1969

## Notes

1. *The Works of Joseph Butler*, ed. W. E. Gladstone, Vol. II (Oxford, 1896), p. 114, n. 1.
2. See Hosea, 6:6.
3. *Merchant of Venice*, Act. III, sc. 1.

# 22

# Adam

Mark 1:12–13

Most of the texts that have been expounded in this series of sermons are hard to take because they disturb our *moral* expectations. The text that I have chosen is, I think, hard to take for two rather different reasons.

In the first place, it is a text that makes extraordinary demands, not so much upon our generosity as upon our imagination. We don't know how to take it, don't know what to do with it. (Later on I shall suggest another reason for its difficulty: namely, in the measure that we *do* discover what to do with it, it is really rather frightening.)

During December and January, my wife and I were travelling in India, where I was giving something called the Teape Lectures. In several cities, we visited both mosques and Hindu temples.

The world of Islam is very different from that of the European Catholic Christianity in which I breathe most easily. Nevertheless, I do not find Islam *unimaginable*. The cool, ascetic regularity of spaces in a mosque, the calligraphic harmony of decoration, suggest a world of discipline and reverence which, though foreign to me, I could, I think, begin to understand.

In a modern Hindu temple, on the other hand, I am quite at sea. I do not know what one would do with the colourful profusion of pot-bellied dignitaries, winged animals, votive offerings and slaughtered goats. Nor is it much help to read the Vedic hymns, with their continual celebration of celestial butter (though the Upanishads make sense). My point is that I do not know how those whose world this is inhabit it. The barrier to comprehension is not ignorance of fact, but failure of imagination.

Now let's go back to those strange pictures with which Mark's announcement of the 'good news' of the Son of God begins.

Two briefly sketched, contrasting images. First, a man emerging from the waters of the Jordan sees 'the heavens torn apart and the Spirit descending like a dove on him; and a voice came from heaven, "You are my Son, the Beloved; with you I am well pleased."'

Do others see what Jesus sees, or is this a private vision? And what is the 'Spirit' that comes down like a dove? How would this gentle fluttering be felt? What is the reader meant to make of this? What are we being asked to see, or hear, to imagine or to understand?

Perhaps one clue might be the contrast between this peaceful, sunlit, blessing or approval, and the energetic starkness of the second figure in the diptych with which it is juxtaposed: 'The Spirit immediately drove him out into the wilderness. He was in the wilderness forty days, tempted by Satan; and he was with the wild beasts; and the angels waited on him.' No dove-like breeze *this* 'Spirit'; something, perhaps, more like the fenland wind.

We can't get round this text by the pretence that, of course, we understand these pictures well enough, but just happen not to share the beliefs that they express. If I do not know what it would be like to hear God's voice, this evening, speaking from the heavens, or to be driven by God's Spirit from Pembroke to the wilderness, then these pictures are words written in a language that I do not understand.

Whether in the case of Hindu temple iconography, or of this diptych at the outset of Mark's gospel, the first step on the road to understanding is simply the admission that this *is* a foreign language; that we don't know what to make of it.

At which point, we have a choice. On the one hand, we can set aside these awkward images as the decorative detritus of thought-worlds not our own, and retain what we think is left: the story of an admirably gentle man who sided with the underdog and got done in by the powers that be.

I know of a Texan who, leaving the cinema recently after seeing *Forrest Gump*, turned to his companion and said: 'Didn't you just see Jesus in him?'

Forget all this stuff about the heavens opening and Satan tempting Jesus in the wilderness. Instead – in a world of terrifying dark complexity, of avarice and AIDS and insecurity, in which the weak are slaughtered by economic systems sprung beyond political control – let's cling for comfort to an image of an innocent and kindly individual.

But, for goodness sake, which of these images is myth: the picture of one driven by the Spirit to the desert, or an ancient Jewish prototype of Forrest Gump?

The attempt to discard the imagery and keep the Gospel is thus self-defeating. The alternative is simply to acknowledge that there is no way round these pictures, put here by Mark as readers' guides. For better or for worse, these pictures tell us how to read what follows. When we read of Jesus preaching to the crowds, healing the sick, engaging in polemic with the Pharisees, wracked with terror in Gethsemane, then we are reading the story of one with whom God is well pleased, the story of one wrestling with Satan in the wilderness.

In other words, the purpose of the images of baptism and temptation is not so much to depict incidents which occur before the public ministry gets under way, but rather to help us understand what, in that ministry, is going on, what is at stake, what forces are engaged.

Let's begin with Adam – which, in the Hebrew Bible, usually means 'Everyman', humanity. Adam, no longer in the quiet of the garden, naming all the animals, but in the wilderness, 'with the wild beasts'. The story that the gospels tell of Jesus is, indeed, the story of one man. But the story of this man, this Jesus, this individual human being, told as the tale of one confessed to be the Christ, the Lord's anointed, God's appearance in the world, thereby becomes the story of one man in whose life and destiny the story of the human race is told, enacted, understood. We do not see him as the Christ unless we see ourselves in him.

Thus, as we contemplate this picture of one tempted, threatened, in the wilderness, we might ask: what kind of company do we, as human beings, keep? By and large, the answer which modern Western culture gives has been: we keep no company; we are on our own – the world our plaything and our property, to do with as we will; the heavens empty spaces full of stars – no point in listening there for messages, or voices, or commands.

Our text, in contrast, sets humankind in context, gives us twofold company to keep. As Karl Barth commented: 'We see him in the proximity of angels and of animals. If we forget that he must remain loyal to the earth, we shall never truly understand him; and even less so if we forget that heaven is above him.'[1]

Moreover, we moderns have seen ourselves as those who get things done, as agents, indeed *sole* agents, in the world. But notice that, in these verses from the gospel, there is nothing Jesus *does*, though things are done to him. He is not portrayed as agent, but as patient: as one driven by the Spirit, tempted by Satan, ministered to by angels.

This is not a narrative of agency; it is a passion narrative, a story of things undergone. And that is the next clue that we need.

It is a commonplace to say that the gospels are best read as passion narratives with prologues. What makes the gospels 'Gospel', or good news, is the proclamation of the crucified and risen one, the turning of the world upon the fulcrum of divine involvement. One question worth asking of almost any passage in the gospels, therefore, is: to what feature of the passion story does this passage point?

Consider, for example, in our text, the ministry of angels. Mark's gospel makes no further mention of this theme. But what is implicit in Mark is made explicit in Luke's gospel, where the motif reappears in the description of Christ's agony in that other wilderness, or garden, which we call Gethsemane: 'Then an angel from heaven appeared to him and gave him strength' (Luke 22:43).

Whether in Mark's version, or in Luke's, or Matthew's, accounts of Christ's temptation have been the gospel text for this first Sunday in Lent since at least the fourth century. From John Chrysostom and Augustine, on down the centuries, a constant theme of Christian preaching on this day has been that we learn from Christ's temptation the manner of our own. The devil, says Chrysostom, brings against 'each . . . one of the Lord's servants' the same seduction of power and wealth and glory that he brought against our 'common Lord'; he does so 'not merely in the wilderness, or upon the mountains, but in the cities, and in the marketplace, and in the very courts of justice'.[2] (Chrysostom was not one for keeping preaching out of politics!)

But if we learn from Christ's temptation the manner of our own, we also learn from what he underwent the forms of God's appearance, the character of his enabling grace; in other words: the manner of the ministry of angels. If this were myth, we might expect God's messengers to spring the trap, to rescue Jesus from the cross and lift the burdens that we bear. This does not happen – to Jesus, or to us. God's presence in the world does not afford escape from pain or darkness, agony, uncertainty, or death. That's not how resurrection works.

So far, I have suggested two clues to the decoding of our text. I have suggested, first, that we should take these images, of baptism and of temptation, as guides to help us read what follows. Secondly, the heart and focus of what follows is Christ's passion, death and resurrection – and it is, above all, to help us read this story that Mark gives us, at the outset, these contrasting images of trial and blessing, radiance and wilderness.

The third clue that we need, to unlock this strange text, is the reminder that each phrase sets up echoes from the Hebrew Scriptures. I shall mention two: the period of 'forty days', and the company of 'wild beasts'.

Even before Lent settled, in the Christian calendar, to exactly forty days duration (not counting Sundays), Christians already understood their annual discipline of preparation in terms of the accounts of Christ's temptation interpreted, in turn, through the 'forty days' that Moses spent alone with God on Sinai (Exodus 34:28) and the 'forty days' that Elijah marched towards the mount of Horeb (1 Kings 19:8).

At first sight, there might seem to be a difference: Moses and Elijah journey through the wilderness to meet, alone, with God, whereas Jesus is driven to meet 'Satan'. But keep Gethsemane and Calvary in mind: here is the end and centre of the wilderness; the dark point of the journey, black night rent by a cry of agony which those around misunderstand as invocation of Elijah. One question we should ponder on, in Lent, is this: in what circumstances might we meet with God, and what would we expect to be the manner of that meeting?

Finally, what about the animals? In Hosea, the promised covenant or treaty between human beings and other living creatures – 'the wild animals, the birds of the air, and the creeping things of the ground' – is an image of God's promised peace: 'I will abolish the bow, the sword, and war from the land; and I will make you lie down in safety' (Hosea 2:18).

In Psalm 91, the road to paradise, the garden from which Adam, who had once named the animals in peace, was 'driven out' – like Jesus, to the wilderness? It is the same verb in the Greek (Genesis 3:24) – this road lies not through covenant but victory: 'For he will command his angels concerning you to guard you in all your ways . . . You will tread on the lion and the adder, the young lion and the serpent you will trample underfoot' (Psalm 91:11, 13).

'And he was with the wild beasts.' That's all Mark says. Did the wild beasts threaten him? Did he tame them, enter into treaty with them, or did he overpower them? The text is silent. He was with the wild beasts. How he was with them, and what came of their meeting, we are not told.

But this is *Mark's* gospel, the gospel whose passion story ends, not with appearances of resurrection, not with foretastes or depictions of God's promised peace, but with the finding of the empty tomb, from which the women who discover it, unnerved by the ministry of angels, 'fled . . . for

terror and amazement had seized them; and they said nothing to any one, for they were afraid' (Mark 16:8). The victory is quietly indicated, not displayed.

Today, at any rate, at Lent's beginning, this typically
Markan reticence seems quite appropriate. Lent is, above
all, a time for realism, for disciplined acknowledgement of
how much more like wilderness than garden is the world
which we inhabit, and construct, and tolerate, and endure.
You might almost say that, during Lent, we hold our breath,
await the Easter breathing of the Spirit that drove Jesus, the
new Adam, to the wilderness; praying that the same Spirit,
which descended upon Jesus at his baptism, may rest, as
promised in our first reading from Isaiah, upon all creation
thus become the garden in which wolf lies down with lamb,
the leopard with the kid – and 'the earth [is] full of the
knowledge of [God] as the waters cover the sea' (Isaiah
11:6, 9).

PEMBROKE COLLEGE, CAMBRIDGE, ON THE FIRST SUNDAY OF LENT,
1995, CONCLUDING A SERIES OF SERMONS ON 'HARD TEXTS'

*Notes*

1. Karl Barth, *Church Dogmatics* III/2 (Edinburgh, 1960), p. 4.
2. *The Sunday Sermons of the Great Fathers*, ed. M. F. Toal, Vol. Two
   (London, 1958), p. 21.

# 23

## Feeding ravens

1 Kings 17:1–24
John 11:17–44

The picture on your chapel card portrays a tranquil scene. St Jerome seated at his desk, the concentrating scholar. Above him on the wall, his cardinal's round hat, emblem of the Latin doctor's dignity and, at his feet, the resting lion. And yet, however suitable this image as an epitome of Magdalene, it is more kind to Jerome than my teachers used to be. They said nice things about Augustine and Chrysostom and Basil, but the impression that they always left of Jerome was of a cantankerous old man best suited to be the butt of criticism.

Things haven't changed. J. N. D. Kelly's life of Jerome describes the cardinal's hat as 'an absurd, and anachronistic, blowing up of his brief secretarial service with Pope Damasus'. (Mind you, something similar could be said of many cardinals' hats, but we had better not go into that.) And as for the lion, so far as I can make out, Jerome acquired his lion by having a legend about some other saint with a vaguely similar name misattributed to him.

Nevertheless, let the lion take us from Dürer's engraving to Psalm 104. This is a celebration of creation: of God's royal governance of a fertile world, a garden-world in harmony. It was Cardinal Newman's favourite psalm, because of the verse 'Man goeth forth to his work and to his labour until the evening.' And, in the night, just before man goes out to work at dawn: 'The young lions roar for their prey, seeking their food from God.'

In this peaceful, fertile land, all things are fed by God.
'You make springs gush forth in the valleys; they flow
between the hills, giving drink to every wild animal . . . By
the streams the birds of the air have their habitation; they
sing among the branches.'

But what would happen if the waters ceased to flow, if the
springs dried up, if the land was struck by drought? 'The
ravens brought him bread and meat in the morning, and
bread and meat in the evening; and he drank from the wadi.
But after a while the wadi dried up, because there was no
rain in the land' (1 Kings 17:6–7).

The wadi and the dry land, water and thirst, food and
famine: throughout the Scriptures, these are, not merely
the tokens and the symbols, but the very forms or sacraments of peace and war, of life and death, of God's appearance and his hiddenness – sometimes in judgement,
sometimes quite unexplained.

There is no trace, in the Scriptures, of the banality, the
cliché-strewn abstractness, which disfigures so much of our
talk of life, and love, and justice. Our mistake, perhaps, is to
suppose the brightness of the world to be imaginable without reference to the dark in which it dawns – unlike the
psalmist, who writes so well about creation's flourishing
because he feels the garden-world's fragility: its vulnerability
to drought and desert storm.

Without in any way compromising the announcement of
God's sovereign faithfulness, and hence the primacy of life
to death, of peacefulness to conflict, daylight over dark, the
Scriptures interweave the strands into a single, sometimes
quite disturbing tapestry.

This is true of both this evening's readings. I asked the
Dean if the first reading could begin at verse 1, rather than
(as the Lectionary suggests) at verse 8, because I wanted to
remind you of how the drought – which caused such suffering to the widow of Zarephath and her son – came about.

At which point, a brief distraction. You will have noticed
that Elijah is fed, at God's command, by ravens. This is surprising, because ravens are scavengers and hence (according to Leviticus) unclean (Leviticus 11:15; Proverbs 30:17).

God, of course, cares for *all* his creatures, whatever their feeding habits. Ravens may be scavengers, not farmers: 'they neither sow nor reap', says Jesus in Luke's gospel, 'they have neither storehouse nor barn, and yet God feeds them' (Luke 12:24; cf. Psalm 147:9).

Let's go back to Elijah. If we focus our attention on the ending of the story – '"See, your son is alive." So the woman said to Elijah, "Now I know that you are a man of God, and that the word of the Lord in your mouth is truth"' (17:24) – it comes across, straightforwardly, as an announcement of the power of God's constitutive and healing Word – a Word that brings order out of chaos, daylight out of darkness, life from death.

If, however, we keep the beginning of the story in mind, things get a little more complicated. Elijah sets up a trial of strength: we'll see which God is stronger – King Ahab's Baal (a rain-god, as I understand) or the God Elijah serves: 'As the Lord the God of Israel lives, before whom I stand, there shall be neither dew nor rain these years, except by my word' (17:1).

In other words, the suffering of the widow of Zarephath, and the fatal illness of her son, are not attributable to what we call 'natural' disaster. The woman and her child are innocent victims, caught up in the struggle between Ahab and Elijah. And, into her house, marches the prophet: '"Bring me a little water in a vessel, so that I may drink." As she was going to bring it, he called to her and said, "Bring me a morsel of bread in your hand"' (17:10–11). Look at it from the widow's point of view: isn't there something of the scavenger, the raven, about this prophet, this witness of the love of God?

The living God gives life, irrigates dry land, makes 'springs gush forth in the valleys'. That Elijah should be required to illustrate this God's boundlessly effective and fruitful generosity by drought – death-dealing for the widow's son – is almost intolerably paradoxical.

And yet, the same paradoxes are in place in our second reading. If we focus our attention on the ending of the story, all is well: 'The dead man came out, his hands and

feet bound with strips of cloth, and his face wrapped in a
cloth. Jesus said to them, "Unbind him, and let him go"'
(11:44). Lazarus alive and free, his sisters' sorrow turned to
joy, the resurrection prefigured and God's power in Christ
dramatically displayed.

But, if we go back ten or eleven verses, things get a little
more complicated. Mary, alerted by Martha, comes out to
meet Jesus: 'When Jesus saw her weeping, and the Jews
who came with her also weeping, he was greatly disturbed in
spirit and deeply moved' (11:33).

Disturbed and moved by what? By sympathy? By sorrow?
By affection? Yes, presumably. But I gather that the experts,
dealing with a difficult Greek word, suggest that Jesus is also
powerfully moved to indignation – shaking with anger, if
you like. Why? Because Jesus meets more in his friend's
death than mere mortality. According to Raymond Brown,
Jesus is 'greatly disturbed . . . and deeply moved' because he
finds himself face to face with the realm of Satan.[1] Lazarus'
death, we might say, is a kind of counter-sacrament of that
deadliness, that absolute, unravelling darkness, out of
which, at the world's creation, God's command draws order,
light and life. It may be out of nothing that the world is
made, but it does not follow that its making is uncostly. And
God said 'Lazarus, come out.'

In other words, what we have here – in a manner characteristic of the Fourth Gospel – is a parable not just of Easter
but also of Good Friday. By all means let us read Lazarus'
return to life in the light of Jesus' resurrection, but only if
we also read 'he was greatly disturbed . . . and deeply
moved' in the light of Gethsemane and the cry on Calvary.
The raising of the dead is no uncostly exercise of power.

'"Where have you laid him?" They said to him, "Lord,
come and see." Jesus wept.'[2] In 1622, John Donne preached
a remarkable sermon on those two words, of which he said:
'There is not a shorter verse in the Bible, nor a larger text.'[3]

The New Testament speaks, on three occasions, of Jesus
as having wept. There were, first, tears shed in what Donne
calls 'a condolency of a human and natural calamity fallen
upon one family; Lazarus was dead.'[4] There were, in the sec-

ond place, tears shed 'prophetically' over the calamity to befall Jerusalem and, thirdly, he interprets Hebrews – 'he offered up prayers with loud cries, and tears' – in reference to Gethsemane and the cross. These he calls Christ's 'priestly' tears.

'Jesus wept.' The tears of this text, of our reading, are, says Donne, 'as a spring, a well, belonging to one household, the sisters of Lazarus: the tears over Jerusalem are as a river, belonging to a whole country; the tears upon the cross are as the sea, belonging to all the world.'[5] On this account, Jesus' tears are set in counterpoint to the water flowing out of Eden: it is God's weeping that creates the world, irrigates the wilderness, transforms the desert into God's good garden.

Unless we would not have it so. 'And when God shall come to that last act . . . when he promises, *to wipe all tears from [their] eyes*, what', asks Donne, 'shall God have to do with that eye that never wept?'[6]

Throughout the sermon, he insists that what he calls 'godly tears' are never *simply* tears of sadness, or contrition; nor are they ever simply tears of happiness or joy: 'true sorrow and true joy', he says, 'are things not only contiguous, but continual; they do not only touch and follow one another in a certain succession, joy assuredly after sorrow, but they consist together, they are all one.'[7]

Nevertheless, it is the desert that is temporary, not the garden; it is drought, not flourishing, that endures only for a time. When Elijah's wadi dried up, the people thirsted. But when, as John Donne says in conclusion, God dries up the fountain of tears, this is because 'all occasion of tears' will have been removed, since all things will be then refreshed by what the Book of Revelation calls 'the water of life, bright as crystal, flowing from the throne of God and of the Lamb' (Revelation 22:1).

MAGDALENE COLLEGE, CAMBRIDGE
7 FEBRUARY 1995

## Notes

1. See Raymond E. Brown, *New Testament Essays* (London, 1965), p. 182.
2. I have quoted this verse (11:34) in RSV, because the NRSV's 'Jesus began to weep' would take the wind out of Donne's sails.
3. *The Sermons of John Donne*, ed. George Potter and Evelyn Simpson, vol. 4 (Berkeley, 1959), p. 325.
4. p. 325.
5. p. 326.
6. p. 331.
7. p. 343.

# 24

# Breathing life

Ezekiel 37:1–14
Romans 8:18–27

Isaac Newton and Karl Barth are not usually associated with one another. But listen to this account, by Barth, of how he spent a few days' holiday in the early summer of 1916: 'I sat under an apple tree and began to apply myself to Romans with all the resources that were available to me at the time.'[1]

No other theological work of the twentieth century has had quite the impact of Barth's commentary on the Epistle to the Romans. Without setting it alongside Newton's *Principia*, we can at least say, of both books, that they made a difference. And both of them started life beneath an apple tree!

When Barth comes to comment on the account we heard just now of all creation and 'ourselves, who have the first fruits of the Spirit', groaning in travail while we await 'the redemption of our bodies' (Romans 8:23), he characteristically lays emphasis upon the materiality and ambiguity of our existence.

'Can any one', he asks, 'rid me of . . . the clear conviction . . . that the story of my life and the history of humanity could be more honestly described if the stomach rather than the head were adopted as the point of departure?'[2] Our story, Barth is convinced, is most truly told as the story of the body, rather than the mind.

The history of the human race is a story about bodies: bodies feeding, slaughtering and celebrating; bodies hungry, bodies stretched out with exhaustion; bodies comforting each other, bodies dancing, bodies racked with pain, bodies in birth pangs and disintegration.

And yet, not only do we usually tell the story with the emphasis elsewhere, but we speak as if we wish that *we* were elsewhere, and were indeed something else, as well. Imagining the ethereal to be more comfortable, we distort Paul's longing for 'redemption *of* our body' into something very different: redemption *from* the body.

Bodies are made of matter. If there's somewhere else to go; if there's more to human history than the story of a stomach, how might we imagine this other side of things? No prizes for guessing what, in our culture, the winning candidate would be: we call it 'spirit'. Splendid. But 'What is Spirit?' This is Karl Barth again: 'According to our normal understanding, Spirit tends to be no more than a mist hanging above a marshy land.'[3]

Matter as thick and fat, particular and coloured. Spirit as thin and gaseous, floating above the marsh in ectoplasmic liberty. Isn't Barth right? When we speak of 'spirits' (except, perhaps, for Gordon's gin) does not our imagination hover somewhere between ouija boards and haunted houses, on the one hand and, on the other, insubstantial movements of the heart and mind?

Let's get back to stomachs, which are (in no small measure) what politics and economics are about. Matter, I said, is thick and fat. But, of course, far too many stomachs are dangerously thin, and empty. That is the agenda of our politics. But church leaders must not mention this. They must stay out of politics and stick to 'spirit': turn aside from stomachs and concentrate on wind. (The late Archbishop Helder Camara, of Recife in Brazil, used to say: 'When I say that the hungry should be fed, they call me a saint. When I ask why they are hungry, they call me a communist.')

You see the problem? By taking 'spirit' as antithesis of 'matter', we not only tear ourselves apart, suppose ourselves construct of two quite different kinds of entity, and thereby depreciate the vulnerable, fragile, most material fact we are, in favour of the mist, of phantasms, of free-floating figments of imagination; but, in doing so, we make it very difficult to read the Scriptures and quite impossible to think of God – for thinking of spirit as 'not-matter' encourages us to think of God, of *Holy* Spirit, as not-matter also: God as ethereal, ephemeral, immaterial, unreal.

The single, simple, central thought I want to offer, this Whitsunday, this celebration of God's Spirit's gift, is that 'spirit' is best thought of not as 'not-matter', but as 'not-death'; not as 'not-stomach', but as celebration, feasting; not as mist hanging 'above a marshy land', but as the marshes' draining, the flowering and fruitfulness of things.

This, surely, is the message of that powerful passage from Ezekiel, that vision of a bleak, dead valley, full of bones. 'Our bones are dried up, and our hope is lost, we are cut off completely' (37:11). God's people are in exile, far from home, cut off from Jerusalem. There is some evidence that, before they were taken to captivity, Ezekiel himself was there, in Palestine, a witness to that last losing struggle. The valley of dry bones is a deserted battlefield. There are, we may suppose, places like this, today, in Bosnia and Iraq.

Even warfare has energy and a kind of life. But it is difficult to imagine a more dead place, a place in which the spirit has been more extinguished, than a desert battlefield strewn with corpses so long dead that the vultures have picked clean the skeletons: 'our bones are dried up'.

It is in this bleak deathscape, then, that Ezekiel sees God's promise doing the impossible: breathing life, making again a people, stomachs, living bodies to be taken home.

The word for breath, or wind, or spirit, here, is the same word that was used in the book of Genesis, in the very making of humankind: 'God formed man of dust from the ground, and breathed into his nostrils the breath of life; and the man became a living being' (Genesis 2:7). And now, in this dead valley of Ezekiel's vision, God breathes again, Adam is made again; men and women walk alive again.

Sometimes, in the Bible, God is thought of as a rock, a stronghold, somewhere to run to, a place of shelter from the storm. But, very often, God's presence and activity, God's life-giving Spirit, is itself the storm – disruptive, disconcerting, unpredictable. God's breath brings life, dissipates the mist's inertia, flattens the windbreaks we erect against vitality.

God's Spirit breathes to life, puts flesh on bones, opens up graves, brings exiles home again. But remember that neither Ezekiel nor his contemporaries envisaged a general resurrection of the dead. Ezekiel's powerful images of contrast tell a people which seemed, as a people, to be dead – vanquished, demoralised, dispirited and far from home – that they will come to life again, walk tall again, be gathered home again, to Palestine.

Christian hope may not be bounded, as Ezekiel's was, by the making and remaking of the world we know, yet this familiar labour – the politics and economics of the struggle for peace and justice, dignity and friendship, food and freedom – remains the stuff, the matter, of the Spirit's breathing.

If it really is with *deadliness*, bleached bones, the withering of friendship, the windless desert of desire's exhaustion, that Spirit is to be contrasted, then it turns out (perhaps to our surprise) that it is not matter that is thick and fat and juicy, particular and many-coloured, the beauty-patterned real thing, but spirit!

Decode the world with the prophets and the gospels as your guide, take seriously our confession of the *Creator Spiritus*, and 'matter' is but mere idea, abstraction's mist, pure possibility for Spirit's scope – pure possibility from which God's Spirit breathes all action, energy, beauty, structure, power; vitality, integrity, kindness, friendship, peace. Matter is mere agenda for God's Spirit's gift.

When 'spirit' is thought of as 'not-matter', then the distinction lies (at least in our imagination) between two kinds of entity – the marshland and the hovering mist, for instance. The biblical distinctions lie, however, not so much between two kinds of thing as between two different stories of the world – a story of all things being brought to life, to peace, to harmony and friendship, and a story of the world unravelling, in darkness, sin and terror, towards disintegration.

There is no doubt, of course, which version we would *pre-*

*fer* to tell, which story we would wish were true, but, whether we turn our gaze inwards – to the confusion that we call our selves – or to the world outside, too much evidence points the bleaker way.

How would one get into a position in which to say, with Paul, 'I consider that the sufferings of this present time are not worth comparing with the glory about to be revealed' (Romans 8:18)? I can just about imagine how some courageous and romantic hero (most certainly not me) might say this of himself, but how could anybody say it of other people's suffering? How could we say this, today, of Bosnia?

Luther's comment on this verse from Romans seems, at least at first sight, to make matters almost worse: 'See how [Paul] contracts the suffering of the world into a single drop and a tiny spark, whilst he expands its glory into a mighty ocean and a blaze of fire.' On which Karl Barth remarked, laconically: 'This astonishing manner of observing the affairs of men requires explanation.'[4]

Luther's image makes no attempt, in fact, to understate the suffering of the world, and he certainly does nothing to 'explain' it. He simply sees the 'spark' of all our pain outflamed by God's love's fire. He sees the shining, risen, of the Crucified.

We might say that Luther reads Romans from the standpoint of the Fourth Gospel: 'When [Judas] had gone out, Jesus said, "Now the Son of man has been glorified, and God has been glorified in him"' (John 13:31); and, a little later on that same dark night: '"so now, Father, glorify me in your own presence"' (John 17:5). Easter does not leave Calvary behind, does not 'explain' Gethsemane. But, in the Spirit's gift, we are enabled to interpret Jesus' journey (and, in its light, our own) as the shining in our world, already, of God's consuming glory.

This is how Karl Barth's commentary goes on:

> No careless attitude towards present tribulation can stand even before the aching of a tooth, and still less before the brutal realities of birth, sickness and death, before the iron reality which governs the broad motions of the lives

of men and the stern destiny of nations. Beneath each slight discomfort, and notably beneath the greater miseries of human life, there stands clearly visible the vast ambiguity of its finiteness.[5]

This 'vast ambiguity' persists, in each of us, and through all the history of the world. We can short-circuit it, surrendering either to despair – 'It was all a dream; there is, in fact, only darkness, pointless violence, and fear' – or to the evasive and egocentric cheerfulness which peddles pretty dreams while other people die.

There is, however, a third possibility: that we may be taught to bear our ambiguity, to learn our time to be the time between, in which 'the whole creation' is 'groaning in labour'. God's utterance and breathing, Word and Spirit, takes the time it makes, and what we learn, in Christ, is how the time it takes is lived, and undergone, as life-breathing birth: 'When a woman is in labour, she has pain, because her hour has come. But when her child is born, she no longer remembers the anguish because of the joy of having brought a human being into the world' (John 16:21).

That time will come and, in the meantime, 'The time in which we live' (this is Karl Barth again) 'bears in its womb the eternal, living, unborn Future',[6] whose name we know already, and in whose gentle breathing we can, even now, begin to sing.

SELWYN COLLEGE, CAMBRIDGE, PENTECOST,
30 MAY 1993

*Notes*

1. Eberhard Busch, *Karl Barth: His Life from Letters and Autobiographical Texts* (London, 1976), p. 97.
2. Karl Barth, *The Epistle to the Romans* (London, 1968), p. 311.
3. *Romans*, p. 312.
4. *Romans*, p. 302.
5. *Romans*, pp. 302–3.
6. *Romans*, p. 306.

# 25

## In search of a body

Exodus 19:1–11
1 Peter 2:1–10

Some fifteen years ago, my wife and I found ourselves eating couscous in a slightly seedy Algerian restaurant in a part of Paris not much given to tourism. My memory of that lunch is still vivid because, although we did not know it then, it was to be the last time that we met the friend who was our host that day: the polymathic French Jesuit, Michel de Certeau. He was, for many years, simultaneously professor of the history of spirituality at the Institut Catholique in Paris and director of studies in social sciences at the École des Hautes Etudes. A man of quite exceptional brilliance, he even, for a few years – somewhat bizarrely, given that he spoke no English and was more or less incapable of plain speech – taught undergraduates at the University of California in San Diego. Since his tragically early death, in 1986, he has become something of a cult figure, especially in the United States.

In a study of sixteenth-and seventeenth-century spirituality entitled *The Mystic Fable*, de Certeau said this: 'Christianity was founded upon *the loss of a body* – the loss of the body of Jesus Christ, compounded with the loss of the "body" of Israel, of a "nation" and its genealogy.'[1] It is, I think, a striking and perceptive image.

It is, in the first place, an image of the empty tomb. '"Woman, why are you weeping?" She said to them, "They have taken away my Lord, and I do not know where they have laid him"' (John 20:13). Christianity was founded upon the loss of a body, the body of Jesus Christ. Christians remain, until the end of time, a people in search of a body; in search of the body of the risen Christ; in search of God's fleshed wisdom, God's housed holiness, in the world.

Christianity was founded upon the loss of a body. 'They have taken away my Lord.' The power of de Certeau's observation derives from the insistent recognition that the loss, the dislocation, upon which Christianity is founded, is, at one and same time, the emptiness of a tomb and an interruption in the story of a people. The drama of the story of the early Church is the drama of a people who are no longer quite sure who they are. Children of Abraham? Yes, of course, but – also, something else. People of Israel? Yes, indeed, and yet – not quite, or not quite in the way they were before. Is Israel's story, Israel's 'genealogy', still ours? Yes, and yet: our story seems both *less* than that – a break of *some* kind has occurred, the faultlines of which are legible throughout the books of the New Testament – and also, in some measure, *more*. There are no boundaries now, to this new people, this strange nation whose story is declared to be, in principle, the history of every tribe and nation of the earth. To search for the body of the risen Christ is to search for a society which would be the reconciliation, in justice and in peace, of all of humankind.

We live in a very strange society, in a culture quite eccentric by the standards of at least three quarters of the history of Christianity. The eccentricity I have in mind is this: it is quite possible, in our society, to come across sane and well-educated people who will tell you, with a straight face, that it is important to keep religion out of politics. This is a sermon, not a seminar, and so I will not stop to try to tease out which is the greater eccentricity: the view of 'politics' which that utterance implies or the understanding of 'religion'.

'Christianity was founded upon . . . the loss of the body of Jesus Christ, compounded with the loss of the "body" of a nation.' The search for the body of the risen Christ, the search that constitutes the life of Christianity, is the search for that polity we call 'God's kingdom'. The question is not *whether* the life of the Church, the practice of discipleship, is or is not a political affair. The question is about the *kind* of politics that is appropriate to such discipleship. And this is not a question we can close; it is not a question to which some single, final, satisfactory answer can be found, once for all time. Christianity was founded upon the loss of a body. That body, the body of the risen Christ, which we confess ourselves to be, remains, at the same time, the unattained, the obscure goal, the content of our quest.

The question as to the kind of politics that is appropriate to discipleship may not be a question to which there is some one, timelessly valid, right answer, but it is certainly a question to which wrong answers may be, and often have been, given. Think of the many dreadful things that have been done under the banner of those rolling phrases from our second reading: 'You are a chosen race, a royal priesthood, a holy nation, God's own people' (2:9). A chosen race, elect, elite, superior. God's own people, so unlike those lesser breeds without the law.

Whenever vocation is thus corrupted into self-assertion – whether of a nation, or a class, or race – the first casualty is the memory of what we were elected for, namely: 'that you may proclaim the mighty acts of him who called you out of darkness into his marvellous light' (2:9). And these were 'people-making' deeds: the setting-free of slaves, the gathering of exiles home again; deeds not of domination, but forgiveness; not of division, but of solidarity.

'You are a chosen race, a royal priesthood, a holy nation, God's own people' – but only on condition: that's what the anti-politics that we call 'politics' forgets. To see this, it is necessary to go back from Peter's letter to the passage he was quoting, that passage from the book of Exodus which we heard first. 'You shall be for me a priestly kingdom and a holy nation.' Yes, indeed, but on condition: 'If you obey my voice and keep my covenant' (19:6, 5): the covenant which brings slaves to freedom, sets prisoners free, calls all of humankind from darkness into light. In other words, the politics appropriate to discipleship are whatever politics – their form will vary with the circumstances – will keep alive the sense of that requirement.

Where the relationships between Christian obedience and the wider society are concerned, the strategies available for the politics of discipleship may be plotted along a line the two ends of which are indicated by two consecutive verses from the Sermon on the Mount. At one end: 'You are the salt of the earth' and, at the other: 'You are the light of the world' (Matthew 5:13, 14). And each strategy, however appropriate in some particular time or place, contains within itself the seeds of its corruption.

'You are the salt of the earth.' The flavour of salt permeates the dish in which it is used. The image is that of Christianity unostentatiously at work, leavening the culture of which it forms a part through innumerable acts of silent sanctity. 'But if salt has lost its taste, how can its saltiness be restored?' I don't think that I am wandering too far from the sense of the text if I suggest that this is what happens when the Gospel is assimilated by the culture which it sought to flavour. This – to give it labels – is the Constantinian or Erastian temptation, the insidious seduction of establishment.

'You are a holy nation, God's own people.' Yes, but this announcement has always to be heard as promise and the ground of duty, not as finished fact, achievement, or the warrant for nationalist or imperial arrogance. Christians remain, until the end of time, a people in search of the body they confess themselves to be, the body of the risen Christ.

'You are the light of the world. A city built on a hill cannot be hidden.' No danger, at this end of the spectrum, of assimilation; of mistaking the culture for the Gospel, the nation for the church. The emphasis now is on distinctness, on Christians as a people set apart, on clear lines firmly drawn between the praise of God and civic piety, revealed truth and worldly wisdom, God's holy people and a sinful world.

This strategy, like the previous one, has both its time and place, its context of appropriate emphasis, and also its element of permanent indispensability. 'You are a holy nation, God's own people.' But now it is the church that hears itself addressed by this announcement, rather than society at

large. And, all too easily, we then forget that it is for the sake
of nothing less than all of humankind that, in the meantime, a particular people is set up to serve. Once again, in
other words, the announcement must be heard as promise,
as the ground of duty, not as finished fact, achievement, or
warrant for theocratic or sectarian self-satisfaction.
Christians remain, until the end of time, a people in search
of the body they confess themselves to be.

Whatever else '*ecclesia semper reformanda*' means, it surely
means that, right across the spectrum of strategies that I
have indicated, the Church has ever and again to be re-
called to this recognition.

'Woman, why are you weeping?' She said to them, 'They
have taken away my Lord, and I do not know where they
have laid him.' Obedience to God's voice, the keeping of
the covenant, is not only compatible with, but requires that,
Mary's weeping does not cease until God's holiness is
housed, God's kingdom come. The great voice from the
throne, at the end of the Book of Revelation, still holds out
to us as future promise the time when humankind 'will be
[God's] people, and God himself will be with them'; the
time when 'mourning and crying and pain will be no more';
the time when God will 'wipe every tear from their eyes'
(Revelation 21:4).

TRINITY HALL, CAMBRIDGE,
9 JUNE 1996

*Note*

1. Michel de Certeau, *The Mystic Fable, vol. I: The Sixteenth and Seventeenth
   Centuries* (Chicago, 1992), p. 81.